A spec...
for the men and women of the
Fellowship of Christian Peace Officers.
These brave men and women serve God
and their fellow men and put their lives
on the line every day.

Let every soul be subject unto the higher powers.
For there is no power but of God: the powers that be are ordained of God.
Whosoever therefore resisteth the power, resisteth the ordinance of God:
and they that resist shall receive to themselves damnation.
For rulers are not a terror to good works, but to the evil.
Wilt thou then not be afraid of the power?
do that which is good, and thou shalt have praise of the same.
(ROMANS 3:1-3)

Studies on
Saving Faith

by

Arthur Pink

Edited by Dr. Don Kistler

Foreword by John MacArthur

The Northampton Press
. . .for instruction in righteousness. . .

The Northampton Press
A division of Don Kistler Ministries, Inc.
P.O. Box 781135, Orlando, FL 32878-1135
www.northamptonpress.org

*

Studies on Saving Faith was first published as a series of articles in
the monthly magazine "Studies in the Scriptures" in 1932,
1933, and 1937. This Northampton Press edition, in which
spelling, grammar, formatting, and syntax changes have been
made, is ©2010 by Dr. Don Kistler

*

ISBN 978-0-9826155-1-5

*

Library of Congress Cataloging in Publication Data

Pink, Arthur Walkington, 1886-1952.
  Studies on saving faith / by A. W. Pink; edited by Don Kistler ;
foreword by John Macarthur.
    p. cm.
  "Studies on Saving Faith" was first published as a series of arti-
cles in the monthly magazine "Studies in the Scriptures" in
1932, 1933, and 1937."
  Includes bibliographical references and index.
  ISBN 978-0-9826155-1-5 (alk. paper)
  1. Faith. 2. Assurance (Theology) 3. Salvation--Christianity. I.
Kistler, Don. II. Title.
  BT771.3.P56 2010
  234--dc22
                                    2010003190

Contents

Part 3: Coming to Christ

Part 4: Assurance

Contents

Part 4: Dialogues

Foreword

Arthur W. Pink's *Studies on Saving Faith* is one of the most potent, far-reaching, insightful works he ever penned, and that is saying quite a lot.

This book was written in 1931–33 and first published in serial form in Pink's monthly magazine, *Studies in the Scriptures*. It reflected Pink's deep concern (and his biblical convictions) about false faith, false evangelism, and false assurance. It was, of course, written long before the so-called lordship controversy. Nevertheless, Pink was clearly prompted by concerns about the same kinds of antinomianism and easy-believism that gave rise to no-lordship theology. He clearly saw those trends in their infancy, and rightly feared they would overtake the evangelical movement, fill the church with false converts, and destroy the evangelical testimony about the life-changing truth of the gospel. When first published, this work was a timely word of prophetic warning; but it is even more relevant and more desperately needed today than it ever was.

"At no point does Satan use his cunning and power more tenaciously, and more successfully, than in getting people to believe that they have a saving faith when they have not," Pink said. He wrote this volume to examine *true* saving faith under the bright light of Scripture, and he thereby exposed several varieties of false faith for what they really are.

From the opening sentences of the book, this is vintage Pink: hard-hitting, sharp-edged, deeply convicting, and powerfully biblical. Pink had a real gift for presenting difficult truths simply enough for anyone to see and understand. In this case, the central thesis he defends is unarguable. If more of his contemporaries had truly listened to the message and taken it to heart, the evangelical movement might have been spared multiple generations of superficiality and confusion.

The current generation needs to hear and embrace Pink's message, too. The face of the church has changed dramatically since Pink's time—and decidedly not for the better. The problems of false assurance, superficial professions of faith, half-hearted commitment to the truth, and frivolous Christianity are greater by magnitudes than when Pink wrote this volume. Yet the underlying error is still the same, and the corrective is more apropos than ever.

Pink acknowledged in the opening paragraphs of this book that he was delivering a hard message, and that many readers might think him "captious" (overly critical), "harsh," and too sarcastic for popular tastes. Readers today, plagued with itching ears and intolerant of unvarnished truth, are probably even more likely to complain about Pink's "tone."

But history has clearly vindicated Pink's stance and proved that the warning he tried to give was by no means too shrill. Still, most of today's mainstream evangelicals are naively unaware of the truths Pink highlighted, and blithely unconcerned about how far their movement has drifted from its own core principles. That fact alone demonstrates irrefutably that Pink was neither too pessimistic in his predictions, too harsh in his condemnations, nor too aggressive in trying to sound the alarm.

It is high time for Christians to hear this message clearly—so I am thankful that The Northampton Press is reprinting it in a quality edition. As you read, I hope you will do so with a sober, humble, teachable heart. I know all who listen rightly will be blessed as much as they are convicted. My prayer for you, dear reader, is that this book will motivate you to think more

seriously than ever about saving faith and the dangers of
spurious or half-hearted belief. My hope also is that you will
become part of a movement to restore a sound understanding of
the gospel and a biblical view of faith to the church, for the sake
of generations yet to come.

John MacArthur

Part 1

The Signs of the Times

1

The Signs of the Times

It is generally recognized that spirituality is at a low ebb in Christendom, and not a few perceive that sound doctrine is rapidly on the wane; yet many of the Lord's people take comfort from supposing that the gospel is still being widely preached and that large numbers are being saved thereby. Alas, their optimistic supposition is ill-founded and sandy-grounded. If the "message" now being delivered in mission halls is examined, if the "tracts" that are scattered among the unchurched masses are scrutinized, if the "open-air" speakers are carefully listened to, if the "sermons" or "addresses" of a "soul-winning campaign" are analyzed; in short, if modern "evangelism" is weighed in the balances of Holy Writ, it will be found wanting—lacking that which is vital to a genuine conversion, lacking what is essential if sinners are to be shown their need of a Savior, lacking that which will produce the transfigured lives of new creatures in Christ Jesus.

It is in no captious spirit that we write, seeking to make men offenders for a word. It is not that we are looking for perfection and complain because we cannot find it, nor that we criticize others because they are not doing things as we think they should be done. No, no, it is a matter far more serious than that. The "evangelism" of the day is not only superficial to the last degree, but it is radically defective. It is utterly lacking a foundation on which to base an appeal for sinners to come to Christ. There is

1

not only a lamentable lack of proportion (the mercy of God being made far more prominent than His holiness, His love more than His wrath), but there is a fatal omission of that which God has given for the purpose of imparting a knowledge of sin. There is not only a reprehensible introducing of bright singing, humorous witticisms and entertaining anecdotes, but there is a studied omission of the dark background upon which alone the gospel can effectually shine forth.

But serious indeed as is the above indictment, it is only half of it—the negative side, that which is lacking. Worse still is that which is being retailed by the cheap-jack evangelists of the day. The positive content of their message is nothing but a throwing of dust in the eyes of the sinner. His soul is put to sleep by the devil's opiate, ministered in a most unsuspecting form. Those who really receive the "message" that is now being given out from most of the "orthodox" pulpits and platforms today are being fatally deceived. It is a way that seems right unto a man, but unless God sovereignly intervenes by a miracle of grace all who follow it will surely find that the ends thereof are the ways of death. Tens of thousands who confidently imagine they are bound for heaven will get a terrible disillusionment when they awake in hell.

What is the gospel? Is it a message of glad tidings from heaven to make God-defying rebels at ease in their wickedness? Is it given for the purpose of assuring the pleasure-crazy young people that, providing they only "believe," there is nothing for them to fear in the future? One would certainly think so from the way in which the gospel is presented—or rather perverted—by most of the "evangelists," and the more so when we look at the lives of their "converts." Surely those with any degree of spiritual discernment must perceive that to assure such that God loves them and His Son died for them, and that a full pardon for all their sins (past, present, and future) can be obtained by simply "accepting Christ as their personal Savior," is but a casting of pearls before swine.

The gospel is not a thing apart. It is not something independent of the prior revelation of God's law. It is not an announcement that God has relaxed His justice or lowered the standard of His holiness. So far from that, when scripturally expounded, the gospel presents the clearest demonstration and the climactic proof of the inexorableness of God's justice, and of His infinite abhorrence of sin. But for scripturally expounding the gospel, beardless youths and businessmen who devote their spare time to "evangelistic efforts" are quite unqualified. Alas, that the pride of the flesh allows so many incompetent ones to rush in where those much wiser fear to tread. It is this multiplying of novices that is largely responsible for the woeful situation now confronting us, and because the "churches" and "assemblies" are so largely filled with their "converts," explains why they are so unspiritual and worldly.

No, dear reader, the gospel is very, very far from making light of sin. The gospel shows us how unsparingly God deals with sin. It reveals to us the terrible sword of His justice smiting His beloved Son in order that atonement might be made for the transgressions of His people. So far from the gospel setting aside the Law, it exhibits the Savior enduring the curse of it. Calvary supplied the most solemn and awe-inspiring display of God's hatred of sin that time or eternity will ever furnish. And do you imagine that the gospel is magnified or God glorified by going to worldlings and telling them that they may be saved at this moment by simply accepting Christ as their personal Savior, while they are wedded to their idols and their hearts still in love with sin? If I do so, I tell them a lie, pervert the gospel, insult Christ, and turn the grace of God into lasciviousness.

No doubt some readers are ready to object to our harsh and sarcastic statements above by asking, when the question was put "What must I do to be saved?" did not an inspired apostle expressly say "Believe on the Lord Jesus Christ and thou shalt be saved?" Can we err, then, if we tell sinners the same thing today? Have we not divine warrant for so doing? True, those words are found in Holy Writ, and, because they are, many superficial and untrained people conclude they are justified in repeating them to all. But let it be pointed out that Acts 16:31 was not addressed to a promiscuous multitude, but to a particular individual, which at once intimates that it is not a message to be indiscriminately sounded forth, but rather a special word to those whose characters correspond to the one to whom it was first spoken.

Verses of Scripture must not be wrenched from their setting, but weighed, interpreted, and applied in accord with their context; and that calls for prayerful consideration, careful meditation, and prolonged study—and it is failure at this point that accounts for these shoddy and worthless messages of this rush-ahead age. Look at the context of Acts 16:31, and what do you find? What was the occasion, and to whom was it that the apostle and his companions said "Believe on the Lord Jesus Christ?" A sevenfold answer is there furnished, that supplies a striking and complete delineation of the character of those to whom we are warranted in giving this truly evangelistic word. As we briefly name these seven details, let the reader carefully ponder them.

1. The man to whom those words were spoken had just witnessed the miracle-working power of God. "And suddenly there was a great earthquake, so that the foundations of the prison were shaken: and immediately all the doors were opened, and every one's bands were loosed" (Acts 16:26).

2. In consequence thereof the man was deeply stirred, even to the point of self-despair. "He drew out his sword and would have killed himself, supposing that the prisoners had been fled" (v. 27).

3. He felt the need of illumination. "Then he called for a light" (v. 29).

4. His self-complacency was utterly shattered, for he "came trembling" (v. 29).

5. He took his proper place (before God)—in the dust, for he "fell down before Paul and Silas" (v. 29).

6. He showed respect and consideration for God's servants, for he "brought them out" (v. 30).

7. Then, with a deep concern for his soul, he asked, "What must I do to be saved?"

Here, then, is something definite for our guidance—if we are willing to be guided. It was no giddy, careless, unconcerned person who was exhorted to "simply" believe; but instead it was one who gave clear evidence that a mighty work of God had already been wrought within him. He was an awakened soul (v. 27). In his case there was no need to press upon him his lost condition, for obviously he felt it; nor were the apostles required to urge upon him the duty of repentance, for his entire demeanor betokened his contrition.

But to apply the words spoken to him unto those who are totally blind to their depraved state and completely dead toward God, would be more foolish than placing a bottle of smelling salts to the nose of one who had just been dragged unconscious out of the water. Let the critic of this article read carefully through the Acts and see if he can find a single instance of the apostles addressing a promiscuous audience or a company of idolatrous heathen and simply telling them to believe in Christ.

Just as the world was not ready for the New Testament before it received the Old, just as the Jews were nor prepared for the ministry of Christ until John the Baptist had gone before Him with his claimant call to repentance, so the unsaved are in no condition today for the gospel till the Law is applied to their hearts, for "by the law is the knowledge of sin" (Romans 3:20). It is a waste of time to sow seed on ground that has never been plowed or spaded! To present the vicarious sacrifice of Christ to those whose dominant passion is to take their fill of sin is to give that which is holy unto the dogs. What the unconverted need to hear about is the character of Him with whom they have to do, His claims upon them, His righteous demands, and the infinite enormity of disregarding Him and going their own way.

The nature of Christ's salvation is woefully misrepresented by the present-day "evangelist." He announces a Savior from hell rather than a Savior from sin. And that is why so many are fatally deceived, for there are multitudes who wish to escape the lake of fire who have no desire to be delivered from their carnality and worldliness. The very first thing said of Him in the New Testament is, "Thou shalt call His name Jesus, for He shall save His people (not "from the wrath to come," but) from their sins" (Matthew 1:21). Christ is a Savior for those realizing something of the exceeding sinfulness of sin, who feel the awful burden of it on their conscience, who loathe themselves for it, who long to be freed from its terrible dominion, and a Savior for no others. Were He to save from hell those who were still in love with sin, He would be the minister of sin, condoning their wickedness and siding with them against God. What an unspeakably horrible and blasphemous thing with which to charge the Holy One!

Should the reader exclaim, "I was not conscious of the heinousness of sin, nor bowed down with a sense of my guilt when

Christ saved me," then I unhesitatingly reply, "Either you have never been saved at all, or you were not saved as early as you supposed."

True, as the Christian grows in grace he has a clearer realization of what sin is—rebellion against God—and a deeper hatred and sorrow for it; but to think that one may be saved by Christ whose conscience has never been smitten by the Spirit, and whose heart has not been made contrite before God, is to imagine something that has no existence whatever in the realm of fact. "They that be whole need not a physician, but they that are sick" (Matthew 9:12). The only ones who really seek relief from the great Physician are they who are sick of sin, who long to be delivered from its God-dishonoring works and its soul-defiling pollutions.

Inasmuch, then, as Christ's salvation is a salvation from sin—from the love of it, from its dominion, from its guilt and penalty—then it necessarily follows that the first great task and the chief work of the evangelist is to preach upon sin, to define what sin (as distinct from crime) really is, to show wherein its infinite enormity consists, to trace out its manifold workings in the heart, to indicate that nothing less than eternal punishment is its desert. Ah, and preaching upon sin—not merely uttering a few platitudes concerning it, but devoting sermon after sermon to explaining what sin is in the sight of God—will not make him popular nor draw the crowds, will it? No, it will not, and, knowing this, those who love the praise of men more than the approbation of God, and who value their salary above immortal souls, trim their sails accordingly. And if someone objects, "But such preaching will drive people away!" I answer, better drive people away by faithful preaching than drive the Holy Spirit away by unfaithfully pandering to the flesh.

The terms of Christ's salvation are erroneously stated by the present-day evangelist. With very rare exceptions he tells his hearers that salvation is by grace and is received as a free gift, that Christ has done everything for the sinner, and nothing remains but for him to "believe," to trust in the infinite merits of His blood. And so widely does this conception now prevail in "orthodox" circles, so frequently has it been dinned in their ears, so deeply has it taken root in their minds, that for one to now challenge it and denounce it is being so inadequate and one-sided as to be deceptive and erroneous, is for him to instantly court the stigma of being a heretic, and to be charged with dishonoring the finished work of Christ by inculcating salvation by works. Yet, notwithstanding, this writer is quite prepared to run that risk.

Salvation is by grace, and by grace alone; for a fallen creature cannot possibly do anything to merit God's approval or earn His favor. Nevertheless, divine grace is not exercised at the expense of holiness, for it never compromises with sin. It is also true that salvation is a free gift, but an empty hand must receive it, and not a hand that still tightly grasps the world! But it is not true that "Christ has done every thing for the sinner." He did not fill His belly with the husks that the swine ate and find them unable to satisfy. He has not turned his back on the far country, arisen, gone to the Father, and acknowledged his sins—those are acts that the sinner himself must perform. True, he will not be saved for the performance of them, yet it is equally true that he cannot be saved without the performing of them—any more than the prodigal could receive the Father's kiss and ring while he still remained at a guilty distance from Him!

Something more than "believing" is necessary to salvation. A heart that is steeled in rebellion against God cannot savingly believe; it must first be broken. It is written, "except ye repent, ye shall all likewise perish" (Luke 13:3). Repentance is just as essential as faith, yea, the latter cannot be without the former: "Repented not afterward, that ye might believe" (Matthew 21:32). The order is clearly enough laid down by Christ: "Repent ye, and believe the gospel" (Mark 1:15). Repentance is sorrowing for sin. Repentance is a heart-repudiation of sin. Repentance is a heart determination to forsake sin. And where there is true repentance grace is free to act, for the requirements of holiness are conserved when sin is renounced. Thus, it is the duty of the evangelist to cry, "Let the wicked forsake his way, and the unrighteous man his thoughts; and let him return unto the Lord (from whom he departed in Adam), and He will have mercy upon him" (Isaiah 55:7). His task is to call on his hearers to lay down the weapons of their warfare against God, and then to sue for mercy through Christ.

The way of salvation is falsely defined. In most instances the modern "evangelist" assures his congregation that all any sinner has to do in order to escape hell and make sure of heaven is to "receive Christ as his personal Savior." But such teaching is utterly misleading. No one can receive Christ as his Savior while he rejects Him as Lord. It is true, the preacher adds, that the one who accepts Christ should also surrender to Him as Lord, but he at once spoils it by asserting that though the convert fails to do so nevertheless heaven is sure to him. That is one of the devil's lies. Only those who are spiritually blind would declare that Christ will save any who despise His authority and refuse His yoke. Why, my reader, that would not be grace but a disgrace—charging Christ with placing a premium on lawlessness.

It is in His office of Lord that Christ maintains God's honor, subserves His government, and enforces His Law; and if the reader will turn to those passages—Luke 1:46, 47; Acts 5:31 (prince and Savior); 2 Peter 1:11; 2:20; 3:18—where the two ti-

tles occur, he will find that it is always "Lord and Savior," and
not "Savior and Lord." Therefore, those who have not bowed to
Christ's scepter and enthroned Him in their hearts and lives,
and yet imagine that they are trusting in Him as their Savior, are
deceived; and unless God disillusions them they will go down to
the everlasting burnings with a lie in their right hand (Isaiah
44:20). Christ is "the Author of eternal salvation unto all them
that obey Him" (Hebrews 5:9), but the attitude of those who do
not submit to His Lordship is "we will not have this Man to
reign over us" (Luke 19:14). Pause, then, my reader, and honestly face the questions: Are you subject to His will? Are you sincerely endeavoring to keep His commandments?

Alas, alas, God's "way of salvation" is almost entirely unknown today, the nature of Christ's salvation is almost universally misunderstood, and the terms of His salvation misrepresented on every hand. The "gospel" that is now being proclaimed is, in nine cases out of every ten, but a perversion of the
truth; and tens of thousands, assured they are bound for
heaven, are now hastening to hell as fast as time can take them.
Things are far, far worse in Christendom than even the "pessi-
mist" and the "alarmist" suppose. I am not a prophet, nor shall I
indulge in any speculation of what Biblical prophecy forecasts—
wiser men than the writer have often made fools of themselves
by so doing. I am frank to say that I do not know what God is
about to do. Religious conditions were much worse, even in
England, one hundred and fifty years ago. But this I greatly fear:
unless God is pleased to grant a real revival, it will not be long
ere "the darkness shall cover the earth, and gross darkness the
people" (Isaiah 60:2), for "evangelism" constitutes, in my judgment, the most solemn of all the "signs of the times."

What must the people of God do in view of the existing
situation? Ephesians 5:11 supplies the divine answer: "Have no

fellowship with the unfruitful works of darkness, but rather re-
prove them," and everything opposed to the light of the Word is
"darkness." It is the bound duty of every Christian to have no
dealings with the "evangelistic" monstrosity of the day, to withhold all moral and financial support of the same, to attend none
of their meetings, to circulate none of their tracts. Those
preachers who tell sinners they may be saved without forsaking
their idols, without repenting, without surrendering to the
Lordship of Christ, are as erroneous and dangerous as others
who insist that salvation is by works and that heaven must be
earned by our own efforts.

Part 2

Saving Faith

2

Saving Faith

"He that believeth and is baptized shall be saved, but he that believeth not shall be damned" (Mark 16:16). These are the words of Christ, the risen Christ, and are the last that He uttered ere He left this earth. None more important were ever spoken to the sons of men. They call for our most diligent attention. They are of the greatest possible consequence, for in them are set forth the terms of eternal happiness or misery, life and death, and the conditions of both. Faith is the principal saving grace, and unbelief is the chief damning sin. The law, which threatens death for every sin, has already passed sentence of condemnation upon all because all have sinned. This sentence is so peremptory that it admits of but one exception—all shall be executed if they do not believe.

The condition of life as made known by Christ in Mark 16:16 is double: the principal one, faith; the accessory one, baptism—accessory, I term it, because it is not absolutely necessary to life, as faith is. Proof of this is found in the fact of the omission in the second half of the verse: it is not "he that is not baptized shall be damned," but, "he that believeth not." Faith is so indispensable that, though one is baptized, yet does not believe, he shall be damned. As I have said above, the sinner is already condemned; the sword of divine justice is drawn even now and waits only to strike the fatal blow. Nothing can divert it but saving faith in Christ. My reader, continuance in unbelief makes hell as certain as though you were already in it. While you remain in unbelief, you have no hope, and are without God in the world (Ephesians 2:12).

Now if believing is so necessary, and unbelief so dangerous and fatal, it deeply concerns us to know what it is to believe. It behooves each one of us to make the most diligent and thorough inquiry as to the nature of saving faith. The more so because all faith does not save; yea, all faith in Christ does not save. Multitudes are deceived upon this vital matter. Thousands of those who sincerely believe that they have received Christ as their personal Savior and are resting on His finished work are building upon a foundation of sand. Vast numbers who have no doubt but that God has accepted them in the Beloved, and are eternally secure in Christ, will only be awakened from their pleasant dreamings when the cold hand of death lays hold of them—and then it will be too late. This is unspeakably solemn. Reader, will that be your fate? Others just as sure they were saved as you are are now in hell.

3

Saving Faith: Its Counterfeits

There are those who have a faith that is so like that which is saving as they themselves may take it to be the very same, and others too may deem it sufficient, yea, even others who have the spirit of discernment. Simon Magus is a case in point. Of him it is written, "Then Simon himself believed also; and when he was baptized, he continued with Philip" (Acts 8:13). Such a faith had he, and so expressed it, that Philip took him to he a genuine Christian, and admitted him to those privileges that are peculiar to them. Yet, a little later, the Apostle Peter said to him, "Thou hast neither part nor lot in this matter; for thy heart is not right in the sight of God . . . I perceive that thou art in the gall of bitterness, and in the bond of iniquity" (Acts 8:21, 23).

A man may believe all the truth contained in Scripture, so far as he is acquainted with it, and he may be familiar with far more than are many genuine Christians. He may have studied the Bible for a longer time, and so his faith may grasp much that they have not yet reached. As his knowledge may be more extensive, so his faith may be more comprehensive. In this kind of faith he may go as far as the Apostle Paul did when he said, "But this I confess unto thee, that after the way which they call heresy, so worship I the God of my fathers, believing all things which are written in the law and in the prophets" (Acts 24:14). But this is no proof that his faith is saving. An example to the

15

contrary is seen in Agrippa. "King Agrippa, believest thou the prophets? I know that thou believest" (Acts 26:27).

Call the above a mere historical faith if you will, yet Scripture also teaches that people may possess a faith that is one of the Holy Spirit, and yet that is a non-saving one. This faith that I now allude to has two ingredients that neither education nor self-effort can produce, spiritual light and a divine power moving the mind to assent. Now a man may have both illumination and inclination from heaven and yet not be regenerated. We have a solemn proof of this in Hebrews 6:4-6. There we read of a company of apostates, concerning whom it is said, "It is impossible to renew them again unto repentance." Yet of these we are told that they were "enlightened," and had "tasted of the heavenly gift," which means that they not only perceived it, but were inclined toward and embraced it—and both because they were "partakers of the Holy Spirit."

People may have a divine faith, not only in its originating power, but also in its foundation. The ground of their faith may be the divine testimony, upon which they rest with unshaken confidence. They may give credit to what they believe not only because it appears reasonable or even certain, but because they are fully persuaded it is the Word of Him who cannot lie. To believe the Scriptures on the ground of their being God's Word is a divine faith. Such a faith the nation of Israel had after their wondrous exodus from Egypt and deliverance from the Red Sea. Of them it is recorded: "The people feared the Lord, and believed the Lord, and His servant Moses" (Exodus 14:31); yet of the great majority of them it is said, "Whose carcasses fell in the wilderness . . . and to whom sware He that they should not enter into His rest" (Hebrews 3:17-18).

It is indeed searching and solemn to make a close study of Scripture on this point, and discover how much is said of unsaved people in a way of having faith in the Lord. In Jeremiah 13:11 we find God saying, "For as the girdle cleaveth to the loins of a man, so have I caused to cleave unto Me the whole house of Israel, and the whole house of Judah, saith the Lord"; and to "cleave" unto God is the same as to "trust" Him (see 2 Kings 18:5-6). Yet of that very same generation God said, "This evil people, which refuse to hear My words, which walk in the imagination of their heart, and walk after other gods, to serve them, and to worship them, shall even be as this girdle, which is good for nothing" (Jeremiah 13:10).

The term "stay" is another word denoting firm trust. "And it shall come to pass in that day, that the remnant of Israel, and such as are escaped of the house of Jacob, shall no more again stay upon him that smote them; but shall stay upon the Lord" (Isaiah 10:20). "Thou wilt keep him in perfect peace, whose mind is stayed on Thee" (Isaiah 26:3). And yet we find a class of whom it is recorded, "They call themselves of the holy city, and stay themselves upon the God of Israel" (Isaiah 48:2). Who would doubt that this was a saving faith? Ah, let us not be too hasty in jumping to conclusions, for of this same people God said, "Thou art obstinate, and thy neck is an iron sinew, and thy brow brass" (Isaiah 48:4).

Again, the term "lean" is used to denote not only trust, but dependence on the Lord. Of the Spouse it is said, "Who is this that cometh up from the wilderness, leaning upon her Beloved?" (Song of Solomon 8:5). Can it be possible that such an expression as this is applied to those who are unsaved? Yes, it is, and by none other than God Himself. "Hear this, I pray you, ye heads of the house of Jacob, and princes of the house of Israel, that abhor judgment, and pervert all equity . . . The heads thereof judge for reward, and the priests thereof teach for hire, and the prophets thereof divine for money; yet will they lean upon the Lord, and say, 'Is not the Lord among us? None evil can come upon us' " (Micah 3:9,11). So thousands of carnal and worldly people are leaning upon Christ to uphold them, so that they cannot fall into hell, and are confident that no "evil" can befall them. Yet is their confidence a horrible presumption.

To rest upon a divine promise with implicit confidence, and that in the face of great discouragement and danger, is surely something that we would not expect to find predicated of a people who were unsaved. Ah, truth is stranger than fiction. This very thing is depicted in God's unerring Word. When Sennacherib and his great army besieged the cities of Judah, Hezekiah said, "Be strong and courageous, be not afraid nor dismayed for the king of Assyria, nor for all the multitude that is with him; for there be more with us than with him. With him is an arm of flesh; but with us is the Lord our God" (2 Chronicles 32:7-8). And we are told that "the people rested themselves upon the words of Hezekiah." Hezekiah had spoken the words of God, and for the people to rest upon them was to rest on God Himself. Yet, less than fifteen years after, this same people did "worse than the heathen" (2 Chronicles 33:9). Thus, resting upon a promise of God is not, of itself, any proof of regeneration.

To rely upon God, on the ground of His "covenant," was far more than resting upon a divine promise; yet unregenerate men may do even this. A case in point is found in Abijah king of Judah. It is indeed striking to read and weigh what he said in 2 Chronicles 13 when Jeroboam and his hosts came up against him. First, he reminded all Israel that the Lord God had given the kingdom to David and his sons forever "by a covenant of salt" (v. 5). Next, he denounced the sins of his adversary (vv. 6-9). Then he affirmed the Lord to be "our God," and that He was with him and his people (vv. 10-12). But Jeroboam did not heed, but forced the battle upon them. "Abijah and his people slew them with a great slaughter" (v. 17), "because they relied upon the Lord God of their fathers" (v. 18). Yet of this same Abijah it is said, "He walked in all the sins of his father" (1 Kings 15:3). Unregenerate men may rely upon God, depend upon Christ, rest on His promise, and plead his covenant.

"The people of Nineveh (who were heathen) believed God" (Jonah 3:5). This is striking, for the God of heaven was a stranger to them, and His prophet a man whom they did not know. Why then should they trust his message? Moreover, it was not a promise, but a threatening that they believed. How much easier then is it for a people now living under the gospel to apply to themselves a promise than the heathen a terrible threat!

David Clarkson, for some time a co-pastor with John Owen, wrote in 1680: "In applying a threatening we are like to meet with more opposition, both from within and from without. From within, for a threatening is like a bitter pill, the bitterness of death is in it; no wonder if that hardly goes down. From without too, for Satan will be ready to raise opposition. He is afraid to have men startled lest the sense of their misery denounced in the threatening should rouse them up to seek how they may make an escape. He is more sure of them while they are secure, and will labor to keep them off the threatening, lest it should awaken them from dreams of peace and happiness, while they are sleeping in his very jaws.

"But now, in applying a promise, an unregenerate man ordinarily meets with no opposition. Not from within, for the promise is all sweetness; the promise of pardon and life is the very marrow, the quintessence of the gospel. No wonder if they are ready to swallow it down greedily. And Satan will be so far from opposing that he will rather encourage and assist one who has no interest in the promise to apply it; for this he knows will be the way to fix and settle them in their natural condition. A promise misapplied will be a seal upon the sepulcher, making them sure in the grave of sin, wherein they lay dead and rotting. Therefore if unregenerate men may apply a threatening, which is in these respects more difficult, as appears they may by the case of the Ninevites, why may they not be apt to apply (appropriate) a gospel promise when they are not like to meet with difficulty and opposition?"

Another most solemn example of those having faith, but not a saving one, is seen in the stony-ground hearers, of whom Christ said, "which for a while believe" (Luke 8:13). Concerning this class the Lord declared that they hear the Word and with joy receive it (Matthew 13:20). How many such have we met and known, happy souls with radiant faces, exuberant spirits, full of zeal that others too may enter into the bliss that they have found. How difficult it is to distinguish such from genuine Christians—the good-ground hearers. The difference is not apparent; no, it lies beneath the surface. They have no root in themselves (Matthew 13:21); deep digging has to be done to discover this fact! Have you searched yourself narrowly, my reader, to ascertain whether or no "the root of the matter" (Job 19:28) is in you?

But let us refer now to another case that seems still more incredible. There are those who are willing to take Christ as their Savior, yet who are most reluctant to submit to Him as their Lord, to be at His command, to be governed by His laws. Yet there are some unregenerate persons who acknowledge Christ as their Lord. Here is the Scripture proof of our assertion: "Many will say to me in that day, 'Lord, Lord, have we not prophesied in Thy name? And in thy name have cast out devils? And in thy name done many wonderful works?' and then will I profess unto them, 'I never knew you; depart from Me, ye that work iniquity'" (Matthew 7:22-23). There is a large class ("many") who profess subjection to Christ as Lord, and who do many mighty works in His name. Thus there is a people who can even show you their faith by their works, and yet it is not a saving one!

It is impossible to say how far a non-saving faith may go, and how very closely it may resemble that faith which is saving. Saving faith has Christ for its object; so has a non-saving faith (John 2:23-24). Saving faith is wrought by the Holy Spirit; so is a non-saving faith (Hebrews 6:4). Saving faith is produced by the Word of God; so also is a non-saving faith (Matthew 13:20-21). Saving faith will make a man prepare for the coming of the Lord, so also will a non-saving. Of both the foolish and wise virgins it is written, "then all those virgins arose, and trimmed their lamps" (Matthew 25:7). Saving faith is accompanied with joy; so also is a non-saving faith (Matt. 13:20).

Perhaps some readers are ready to say that all of this is very unsettling, and, if really heeded, most distressing. May God in His mercy grant that this article may have just these very effects on many who read it. Oh, if you value your soul, do not dismiss it lightly. If there is such a thing (and there is) as a faith in Christ that does not save, then how easy it is to be deceived about my faith! It is not without reason that the Holy Spirit has so plainly cautioned us at this very point. "A deceived heart hath turned him aside" (Isaiah 44:20). "The pride of thine heart hath deceived thee" (Obadiah 3). "Take heed that ye be not deceived" (Luke 21:8). "For if a man think himself to be something, when he is nothing, he deceiveth himself" (Galatians 6:3). At no point does Satan use his cunning and power more tenaciously, and more successfully, than in getting people to believe that they have a saving faith when they do not.

The devil deceives more souls by this one thing than by all his other devices put together. Take this present article as an illustration. How many a Satan-blinded soul will read it and then say, "It does not apply to me. I know that my faith is a saving one!" It is in this way that the devil turns aside the sharp point of God's convicting Word, and secures his captives in their unbelief. He works in them a sense of false security by persuading them that they are safe within the ark, and induces them to ignore the threatenings of the Word and appropriate only its comforting promises. He dissuades them from heeding that most salutary exhortation, "Examine yourselves, whether ye be in the faith; prove your own selves" (2 Corinthians 13:5). Oh, my reader, heed that word now.

In closing this first article I will endeavor to point out some of the particulars in which this non-saving faith is defective, and wherein it comes short of a faith that does save. First, with many it is because they are willing for Christ to save them from hell, but are not willing for Him to save them from self. They want to be delivered from the wrath to come, but they wish to retain their self-will and self-pleasing. But He will not be dictated unto. You must be saved on His terms, or not at all. When Christ saves, He saves from sin—from its power and pollution, and therefore from its guilt. And the very essence of sin is the determination to have my own way (Isaiah 53:6). Where Christ saves, He subdues the spirit of self-will and implants a genuine, a powerful, a lasting desire and determination to please Him.

Again, many are never saved because they wish to divide Christ; they want to take Him as a Savior, but are unwilling to subject themselves unto Him as their Lord. Or, if they are prepared to own Him as Lord, it is not as an absolute Lord. But this cannot be. Christ will either be Lord of all, or He will not be Lord at all. But the vast majority of professing Christians would have Christ's sovereignty limited at certain points; it must not entrench too far upon the liberty that some worldly lust or carnal interest demands. They covet His peace, but His "yoke" is unwelcome. Of all such Christ will yet say, "But those mine enemies, which would not that I should reign over them, bring hither, and slay them before me" (Luke 19:27).

Again, there are multitudes that are quite ready for Christ to justify them, but not to sanctify. Some kind of, some degree of sanctification, they will tolerate, but to be sanctified wholly, their "whole spirit and soul and body" (1 Thessalonians 5:23), they have no relish for. For their hearts to be sanctified, for pride and covetousness to be subdued, would be too much like the plucking out of a right eye. For the constant mortification of all their members, they have no taste. For Christ to come to them as a Refiner, to burn up their lusts, consume their dross, to utterly dissolve their old frame of nature, to melt their souls, so as to make them run in a new mould, they do not like. To utterly deny self, and take up their cross daily, is a task from which they shrink with abhorrence.

Again, many are willing for Christ to officiate as their Priest, but not for Him to legislate as their King. Ask them, in a general way, if they are ready to do whatsoever Christ requires of them, and they will answer in the affirmative, emphatically and with confidence. But come to particulars; apply to each one of them those specific commandments and precepts of the Lord that they are ignoring, and they will at once cry out "Legalism!" or, "We cannot be perfect in everything." Name nine duties, and perhaps they are performing them, but mention a tenth and it at once makes them angry, for you have come too close home to their case. Herod heard John gladly and did "many things" (Mark 6:20), but when he referred to Herodias, he touched him to the quick. Many are willing to give up their going to the theater, and their card parties, who refuse to go forth unto Christ outside the camp. Others are willing to go outside the camp, yet refuse to deny their fleshly and worldly lusts. Reader, if there is a reserve in your obedience, you are on the way to hell. My next article will take up the nature of saving faith.

4

Saving Faith: Its Nature

"There is a generation that are pure in their own eyes, and yet is not washed from their filthiness" (Proverbs 30:12). A great many suppose that such a verse as this applies only to those who are trusting in something other than Christ for their acceptance before God, such as people who are relying upon baptism, church membership, or their own moral and religious performances. But it is a great mistake to limit such scriptures unto the class just mentioned. Such a verse as, "There is a way which seemeth right unto a man, but the end thereof are the ways of death" (Proverbs 14:12) has a far wider application than merely to those who are resting on something of or from themselves to secure a title to everlasting bliss. Equally wrong is it to imagine that the only deceived souls are they who have no faith in Christ.

There is in Christendom today a very large number of people who have been taught that nothing the sinner can do will ever merit the esteem of God. They have been informed, and rightly so, that the highest moral achievements of the natural man are only "filthy rags" in the sight of the thrice holy God. They have heard quoted so often such passages as, "By grace are ye saved through faith, and that not of yourselves; it is the gift of God, not of works, lest any man should boast" (Ephesians 2:8–9), and, "Not by works of righteousness which we have done, but according to His mercy He saved us" (Titus 3:5), that they

have become thoroughly convinced that heaven cannot be attained by any doing of the creature. Further, they have been told
so often that Christ alone can save any sinner that this has become a settled article in their creed, from which neither man
nor devil can shake them. So far so good.

That large company to whom we are now referring have also
been taught that while Christ is the only way unto the Father,
yet He becomes so only as faith is personally exercised in and
upon Him, that He becomes our Savior only when we believe
on Him. During the last twenty-five years, almost the whole emphasis of "gospel preaching" has been thrown upon faith in
Christ, and evangelistic efforts have been almost entirely confined to getting people to "believe" on the Lord Jesus. Apparently there has been great success; thousands upon thousands
have responded; they have, as they suppose, accepted Christ as
their own personal Savior. Yet I wish to point out here that it is
as serious an error to suppose that all who "believe in Christ"
are saved as it is to conclude that only those are deceived (and
are described in Proverbs 14:12 and 30:12) who have no faith in
Christ.

No one can read the New Testament attentively without discovering that there is a "believing" in Christ that does not save.
In John 8:30 we are told, "As He spake these words, many believed on Him." Mark carefully, it is not said "many believed *in*
Him," but "many believed *on* Him." Nevertheless one does not
have to read much farther in the chapter to discover that those
very people were unregenerate and unsaved souls. In verse 44 we
find the Lord telling these very "believers" that they were of
their father the devil; and in verse 59 we find them taking up
stones to cast at Him. This has presented a difficulty unto some;
yet it ought not do so. They created their own difficulty by supposing that all faith in Christ necessarily saves. It does not.

There is a faith in Christ that saves, and there is also a faith in Christ that does not save.

"Among the chief rulers also many believed on Him." Were, then, those men saved? Many preachers and evangelists, as well as tens of thousands of their blinded dupes, would answer, "Most assuredly." But let us note what immediately follows here: "but because of the Pharisees they did not confess Him, lest they should be put out of the synagogue; for they loved the praise of men more than the praise of God" (John 12:42-43). Will any of my readers now say that those men were saved? If so, it is clear proof that you are utter strangers to any saving work of God in your own souls. Men who are afraid to hazard the loss of their worldly positions, temporal interests, personal reputations, or anything else that is dear to them for Christ's sake are yet in their sins—no matter how they may be trusting in Christ's finished work to take them to heaven.

Probably most of my readers have been brought up under the teaching that there are only two classes of people in this world, believers and unbelievers. But such a classification is most misleading, and is utterly erroneous. God's Word divides earth's inhabitants into three classes: "Give none offence, neither to [1] the Jews, nor [2] to the Gentiles, nor [3] to the church of God" (1 Corinthians 10:32). It was so during Old Testament times, more noticeably so from the days of Moses onwards. There were first the "gentile" or heathen nations, outside the commonwealth of Israel, which formed by far the largest class. Corresponding with that class today are the countless millions of modern heathen who are "lovers of pleasure more than lovers of God." Second, there was the nation of Israel, which has to be subdivided into two groups, for, as Romans 9:6 declares, "They are not all Israel, which are of Israel." By far the larger portion of the nation of Israel were only the nominal people of God, in outward relation to Him; corresponding with this class is the great mass of professors bearing the name of Christ. Third, there was the spiritual remnant of Israel, whose calling, hope, and inheritance were heavenly; corresponding to them this day are the genuine Christians, God's "little flock" (Luke 12:32).

The same threefold division among men is plainly discernible throughout John's Gospel. First, there were the hardened leaders of the nation, the scribes and Pharisees, priests and elders. From start to finish they were openly opposed to Christ, and neither His blessed teaching nor His wondrous works had any melting effects upon them. Second, there were the common people who "heard Him gladly" (Mark 12:37), a great many of whom are said to have "believed on Him" (see John 2:23; 7:31; 8:30; 10:42; and 12:11), but concerning whom there is nothing to show that they were saved. They were not outwardly opposed to Christ, but they never yielded their hearts to Him. They were impressed by His divine credentials, yet were easily offended (John 6:66). Third, there was the insignificant handful who "received Him" (John 1:12) into their hearts and lives, received Him as their Lord and Savior.

The same three classes are clearly discernible (to anointed eyes) in the world today. First, there are the vast multitudes who make no profession at all, who see nothing in Christ that they should desire Him; people who are deaf to every appeal, and who make little attempt to conceal their hatred of the Lord Jesus. Second, there is that large company who are attracted by Christ in a natural way. So far from being openly antagonistic to Him and His cause, they are found among His followers. Having been taught much of the truth, they "believe in Christ," just as children reared by conscientious Mohammedans believe firmly and devoutly in Mohammed. Having received much instruction concerning the virtues of Christ's precious blood, they trust in its merits to deliver them from the wrath to come; and yet there is nothing in their daily lives to show that they are new creatures in Christ Jesus! Third, there are the "few" (Matthew 7:13-14) who deny themselves, take up the cross daily, and follow a despised and rejected Christ in the path of loving and unreserved obedience unto God.

Yes, there is a faith in Christ that saves, but there is a faith in Christ that does not save. Probably few will dissent from this statement, yet many will be inclined to weaken it by saying that the faith in Christ that does not save is merely a historical faith, or where there is a believing *about* Christ instead of a believing *in* Him. Not so. That there are those who mistake a historical faith about Christ for a saving faith in Christ I do not deny; but what I would emphasize here is the solemn fact that there are also some who have more than a historical faith, more than a mere head-knowledge about Him, who yet have a faith that comes short of being a quickening and saving one. Not only are there some with this non-saving faith, but today there are vast numbers of such all around us. They are people who furnish the antitypes of those to which we called attention in the last article, who were represented and illustrated in Old Testament times by those who believed in, rested upon, leaned upon, and relied upon the Lord, but who were, nevertheless, unsaved souls.

What then does saving faith consist of? In seeking to answer this question my present object is to supply not only a scriptural definition, but one that, at the same time, differentiates it from a non-saving faith. Nor is this any easy task, for the two things often have much in common. That faith in Christ that does not save has in it more than one element or ingredient of that faith that vitally unites the soul to Him. Those pitfalls that the writer must now seek to avoid are undue discouraging of real saints on the one hand by raising the standard higher than Scripture has raised it, and encouraging unregenerate professors on the other hand by so lowering the standards as to include them. I do not wish to withhold from the people of God their legitimate portion; nor do I want to commit the sin of taking the children's bread and casting it to the dogs. May the Holy Spirit Himself deign to guide us into the truth.

Much error would be avoided on this subject if due care were taken to frame a scriptural definition of unbelief. Again and again in Scripture we find believing and not believing placed in antithesis, and we are afforded much help toward arriving at a correct conception of the real nature of saving faith when we obtain a right understanding of the character of unbelief. It will at once be discovered that saving faith is far more than a hearty assenting unto what God's Word sets before us, when we perceive that unbelief is much more than an error or judgment or a failure to assent unto the truth. Scripture depicts unbelief as a virulent and violent principle of opposition to God. Unbelief has both a passive and active, a negative and positive, side, and therefore the Greek noun is rendered both by "unbelief" (Romans 11:20; Hebrews 4:6, 11) and "disobedience" (Ephesians 2:2; 5:6), and the verb by "believed not" (Hebrews 3:18; 11:31) and "obey not" (1 Peter 3:1; 4:17). A few concrete examples will make this plainer.

Take first the case of Adam. There was something more than a mere negative failing to believe God's solemn threat that in the day he ate of the forbidden fruit he would surely die: by one man's disobedience many were made sinners (Romans 5:19). Nor did the heinousness of our first parent's sin consist in listening to the lie of the serpent, for 1 Timothy 2:14 expressly declares "Adam was not deceived." No, he was determined to have his own way, no matter what God had prohibited and threatened. Thus, the very first case of unbelief in human history consisted not only in negatively failing to take to heart what God has so clearly and so solemnly said, but also in a deliberate defiance of and rebellion against Him.

Take the case of Israel in the wilderness. Concerning them it is said, "They could not enter in [the promised land] because of unbelief" (Hebrews 3:19). Now exactly what do those words signify? Do they mean that Canaan was missed by them because of their failure to appropriate the promise of God? Yes, for a "promise" of entering in was "left" them, but it was not "mixed with faith in them that heard it" (Hebrews 4:1-2). God had declared that the seed of Abraham would inherit that land which flowed with milk and honey, and it was the privilege of that generation which was delivered from Egypt to lay hold of and apply that promise to themselves. But they did not. Yet that is not all! There was something far worse. There was another element in their unbelief that is usually lost sight of nowadays—they were openly disobedient against God. When the spies brought back a sample of the goodly grapes, and Joshua urged them to go up and possess the land, they would not. Accordingly Moses declared, "notwithstanding ye would not go up, but rebelled against the commandment of the Lord your God" (Deuteronomy 1:26). Ah, there is the positive side of their unbelief; they were self-willed, disobedient, and defiant.

Consider now the case of that generation of Israel which was in Palestine when the Lord Jesus appeared among them as "a minister of the circumcision for the truth of God" (Romans 15:8). John 1:11 informs us, "He came unto His own and His own received Him not," which the next verse defines as "they believed" Him not. But is that all? Were they guilty of nothing more than a failure to assent to His teaching and trust in His person? Nay, verily, that was merely the negative side of their unbelief. Positively, they "hated" Him (John 15:25), and would "not come to" Him (John 5:40). His holy demands did not suit their fleshly desires, and therefore they said, "We will not have this man to reign over us" (Luke 19:14). Thus their unbelief, too, consisted in the spirit of self-will and open defiance, a determination to please themselves at all costs.

Unbelief is not simply an infirmity of fallen human nature, it is a heinous crime. Scripture everywhere attributes it to love of sin, obstinacy of will, and hardness of heart. Unbelief has its root in a depraved nature, in a mind that is at enmity against God. Love of sin is the immediate cause of unbelief. "And this is the condemnation, that light is come into the world, and men loved darkness rather than light, because their deeds were evil" (John 3:19). As John Owen wrote: "The light of the gospel is brought unto a place or people; they come so near it as to discover its end or tendency; but as soon as they find that it aims to part them and their sins, they will have no more to do with it. They like not the terms of the gospel, and so perish in and for their iniquities." If the gospel were more clearly and faithfully preached, fewer would profess to believe it!

Saving faith, then, is the opposite of damning belief. Both issue from the heart that is alienated from God, which is in a state of rebellion against Him; saving faith comes forth from a heart that is reconciled to Him, and so has ceased to fight against Him. Thus an essential element or ingredient in saving faith is a yielding to the authority of God, a submitting of myself to His rule. It is very much more than my understanding assenting and my will consenting to the fact that Christ is a Savior for sinners, and that He stands ready to receive all who trust Him. To be received by Christ I must not only come to Him renouncing all my own righteousness (Romans 10:3), as an empty-handed beggar (Matthew 19:21), but I must also forsake my self-will and rebellion against Him (Psalm 2:11–12; Proverbs 28:13).

Should an insurrectionist and seditionist come to an earthly king seeking his sovereign favor and pardon, then, obviously, the very law of his coming to him for forgiveness requires that he should come on his knees, laying aside his hostility. So it is with a sinner who really comes savingly to Christ for pardon; it is against the law of faith to do otherwise.

Saving faith is a genuine coming to Christ (Matthew 11:28; John 6:37). But let us take care that we do not miss the clear and inevitable implication of this term. If I say, "I come to the USA," then I necessarily indicate that I left some other country to get here. Thus it is in coming to Christ; something has to be left. Coming to Christ not only involves the abandoning of every false object of confidence, it also includes and entails the forsaking of all other competitors for my heart. "For ye were as sheep going astray; but are now returned unto the Shepherd and Bishop of your souls" (1 Peter 2:25). And what is meant by "ye were [note the past tense—they are no longer doing so] as sheep going astray"? Isaiah 53:6 tells us: "All we like sheep have gone astray; we have turned every one to his own way." Ah, that is what must be forsaken before we can truly come to Christ—that course of self-will must be abandoned. The prodigal son could not come to his father while he remained in the far country. Dear reader, if you are still following a course of self-pleasing, you are only deceiving yourself if you think you have come to Christ.

Nor is the brief definition that I have given above of what it means really to come to Christ any forced or novel one of my own. In his book *Come and Welcome to Jesus Christ*, John Bunyan wrote: "Coming to Christ is attended with an honest and sincere forsaking all for Him [here he quotes Luke 14:26-27]. By these and like expressions elsewhere, Christ describeth the true comer: he is one that casteth all behind his back. There are a great many pretended comers to Jesus Christ in the world. They are much like the man you read of in Matthew 21:30, that said to his father's bidding, 'I go, sir,' and went not. When Christ calls by His gospel, they say, 'I come, Sir,' but they still abide by their pleasure and carnal delights."

Charles Spurgeon, in a sermon on John 6:44, said, "Coming to Christ embraces in it repentance, self-abnegation, and faith in the Lord Jesus, and so sums within itself all those things that are the necessary attendants of those great steps of heart, such as the belief of the truth, earnest prayers to God, the submission of the soul to the precepts of His Gospel." In his sermon on John 6:37, he says, "To come to Christ signifies to turn from sin and to trust in Him. Coming to Christ is a leaving of all false confidences, a renouncing of all love to sin and a looking to Jesus as the solitary pillar of our confidence and hope."

Saving faith consists of the complete surrender of my whole being and life to the claims of God upon me. "But first gave their own selves to the Lord" (2 Corinthians 8:5).

It is the unreserved acceptance of Christ as my absolute Lord, bowing to His will and receiving His yoke. Possibly someone may object, "Then why are Christians exhorted as they are in Romans 12:1?"

I answer, all such exhortations are simply a calling on them to continue as they began. "As ye have therefore received Christ Jesus the Lord, so walk ye in Him" (Colossians 2:6). Yes, mark it well that Christ is received as Lord. Oh, how far, far below the New Testament standard is this modern way of begging sinners to receive Christ as their own personal "Savior." If the reader will consult his concordance, he will find that in every passage where the two titles are found together it is always "Lord and Savior, and never vice versa. See Luke 1:46-47; 2 Peter 1:11; 2:20; 3:18.

Until the ungodly are sensible of the exceeding sinfulness of their vile course of self-will and self-pleasing, until they are genuinely broken down and penitent over it before God, until they are willing to forsake the world for Christ, until they have resolved to come under His government, for such to depend upon Him for pardon and life is not faith, but blatant presumption; it is but to add insult to injury. And for any such to take His holy name upon their polluted lips and profess to be His followers is the most terribly blasphemy, and comes perilously nigh to committing that sin for which there is no forgiveness. Alas, alas, that type of modern evangelism is encouraging and producing just such hideous and Christ-dishonoring monstrosities.

Saving faith is a believing on Christ with the heart. "If thou shalt confess with thy mouth the Lord Jesus, and shalt believe in thine heart that God hath raised Him from the dead, thou shalt be saved. For with the heart man believeth unto righteousness" (Romans 10:9-10). There is no such thing as a saving faith in Christ where there is no real love for Him, and by "real love" I mean a love that is evidenced by obedience. Christ acknowledges none to be His friends save those who do whatsoever He commands them (John 15:14). As unbelief is a species of rebellion, so saving faith is a complete subjection to God. Hence we read of "the obedience of faith" (Romans 16:26). Saving faith is to the soul what health is to the body: it is a mighty principle of operation, full of life, ever working, bringing forth fruit after its own kind.

5

Saving Faith: Its Difficulty

Some of my readers will probably be surprised to hear about the difficulty of saving faith. On almost every side today it is being taught, even by men called "orthodox" and "fundamentalists," that getting saved is an exceedingly simple affair. So long as a person believes John 3:16, and "rests on it," or "accepts Christ as his personal Savior," that is all that is needed. It is often said that there is nothing left for the sinner to do but direct his faith toward the right object; just as a man trusts his bank or a wife her husband, let him exercise the same faculty of faith and trust in Christ. So widely has this idea been received that for anyone now to condemn it is to court being branded as a heretic. Notwithstanding, this writer here unhesitatingly denounces it as a most God-insulting lie of the devil. A natural faith is sufficient for trusting a human object; but a supernatural faith is required to trust savingly in a divine object.

While observing the methods employed by present-day "evangelists" and "personal workers," we are made to wonder what place the Holy Spirit has in their thoughts; certainly they entertain the most degrading conception of that miracle of grace that He performs when He moves a human heart to surrender truly unto the Lord Jesus. Alas, in these degenerate times few have any idea that saving faith is a miraculous thing. Instead, it is now almost universally supposed that saving faith is nothing more than an act of the human will, which any man is capable of performing. All that is needed is to bring before a sinner a few verses of Scripture that describe his lost condition, one or two that contain the word "believe," and then a little persuasion for him to "accept Christ," and the thing is done. And the awful thing is that so very, very few see anything wrong with this. They are blind to the fact that such a process is only the devil's drug to lull thousands into a false peace.

So many have been argued into believing that they are saved. In reality, their "faith" sprang from nothing better than a superficial process of logic. Some "personal worker" addresses a man who has no concern whatever for the glory of God and no realization of his terrible hostility against Him. Anxious to "win another soul to Christ," he pulls out his New Testament and reads to him 1 Timothy 1:15. The worker says, "You are a sinner," and, his man assenting, he is at-once informed, "Then that verse includes you." Next John 3:16 is read, and the question is asked, "Whom does the word 'whosoever' include?" The question is repeated until the poor victim answers, "You, me, and everybody." Then he is asked, "Will you believe it, believe that God loves you, that Christ died for you?" If the answer is "Yes," he is at once assured that he is now saved. Ah, my reader, if this is how you were "saved," then it was with "enticing words of man's wisdom" and your "faith" stands only "in the wisdom of men" (1 Corinthians 2:4–5), and not in the power of God!

Multitudes seem to think that it is about as easy for a sinner to purify his heart (James 4:8) as it is to wash his hands; to admit the searching and flesh-withering light of divine truth into the soul as the morning sun into his room by pulling up the blinds; to turn from idols to God, from the world to Christ, from sin to holiness, as to turn a ship right round by the help of her helm. Oh, my reader, do not be deceived on this vital matter; to mortify the lusts of the flesh, to be crucified unto the world, to overcome the devil, to die daily unto sin and live unto righteousness, to be meek and lowly in heart, trustful and obedient, pious and patient, faithful and uncompromising, loving and gentle, in a word, to be a Christian, to be Christ-like, is a task far, far beyond the poor resources of fallen human nature.

It is because a generation has arisen which is ignorant of the real nature of saving faith that they deem it such a simple thing. It is because so very few have any scriptural conception of the character of God's great salvation that the delusions referred to above are so widely received. It is because so very few realize what they need saving from that the popular "evangel" of the hour is so eagerly accepted. Once it is seen that saving faith consists of very much more than believing that "Christ died for me," that it involves and entails the complete surrender of my heart and life to His government, few will imagine that they possess it. Once it is seen that God's salvation is not only a legal but also an experimental thing, that it not only justifies but regenerates and sanctifies, fewer will suppose they are its participants. Once it is seen that Christ came here to save His people not only from hell, but from sin, from self-will and self-pleasing, then fewer will desire His salvation.

The Lord Jesus did not teach that saving faith was a simple matter. Far from it! Instead of declaring that the saving of the soul was an easy thing, in which many would participate, He said, "Strait is the gate, and narrow is the way, which leadeth unto life, and few there be that find it" (Matthew 7:14). The only path that leads to heaven is a hard and laborious one. "We must through much tribulation enter into the kingdom of God" (Acts 14:22). An entrance into that path calls for the utmost endeavors of soul. "Strive to enter in at the strait gate" (Luke 13:24).

After the young ruler had departed from Christ, sorrowing, the Lord turned to His disciples and said, "How hard is it for them that trust in riches to enter into the kingdom of God! It is easier for a camel to go through the eye of a needle than for a rich man to enter into the kingdom of God" (Mark 10:24-25). What place is given to such a passage as this in the theology (if "theology" it is fit to be called) that is being taught in the "Bible institutes" to those seeking to qualify for evangelistic and personal work? None at all. According to their views, it is just as easy for a millionaire to be saved as it is for a pauper, since all that either has to do is "rest on the finished work of Christ." But those who are wallowing in wealth do not think of God. "According to their pasture, so were they filled; they were filled, and their heart was exalted; therefore have they forgotten Me!" (Hosea 13:6).

When the disciples heard these words of Christ's "they were astonished out of measure, saying among themselves, 'Who then can be saved?' " Had our modern evangelists heard them, they would soon have set their fears at rest, and assured them that anybody and everybody could be saved if they believed on the Lord Jesus. But Christ did not so reassure them. Instead, He immediately added, "With men it is impossible, but not with God" (Mark 10:27). Of himself, the fallen sinner can no more repent evangelically, believe in Christ savingly, come to Him effectually, than he can create a world. "With men it is impossible" rules out of court all special pleading for the power of man's will. Nothing but a miracle of grace can lead to the saving of any sinner.

And why is it impossible for the natural man to exercise saving faith? Let the answer be drawn from the case of this young ruler. He departed from Christ sorrowing, "for he had great possessions." He was wrapped up in them. They were his idols.

His heart was chained to the things of earth. The demands of Christ were too exacting; to part with all and follow Him was more than flesh and blood could endure. Reader, what are your idols? To him the Lord said, "One thing thou lackest." What was it? A yielding to the imperative requirements of Christ, a heart surrendered to God. When the soul is stuffed with the dregs of earth, there is no room for the impressions of heaven. When a man is satisfied with carnal riches, he has no desire for spiritual riches.

The same sad truth is brought out again in Christ's parable of the "great supper." The feast of divine grace is spread, and through the gospel a general call is given for men to come and partake of it. And what is the response? This: "They all with one consent began to make excuse" (Luke 14:18). And why should they? Because they were more interested in other things. Their hearts were set upon land (verse 18), oxen (verse 19), and domestic comforts (verse 20). People are willing to "accept Christ" on their own terms, but not on His. What His terms are is made known in the same chapter—giving Him the supreme place in our affections (verse 26), the crucifixion of self (verse 27), and the abandonment of every idol (verse 33). Therefore He asked, "Which of you, intending to build a tower [a figure of a hard task of setting the affections on things above], sitteth not down first, and counteth the cost?" (Luke 14:28).

"How can ye believe, which receive honor one of another, and seek not the honor that cometh from God only?" (John 5:44). Do these words picture the exercise of saving faith as the simple matter which so many deem it? The word "honor" here signifies approbation or praise. While those Jews were making it their chief aim to win and hold the good opinion of each other, and were indifferent to the approval of God, it was impossible that they could come to Christ. It is the same now. "Whosoever therefore will be [desires and is determined to be] a friend of the world is the enemy of God" (James 4:4). To come to Christ effectually, to believe on Him savingly, involves turning our backs upon the world, alienating ourselves from the esteem of our godless (or religious) fellows, and identifying ourselves with the despised and rejected One. It involves bowing to His yoke, surrendering to His lordship, and living henceforth for His glory. And that is no small task.

"Labor not for the meat which perisheth, but for that meat which endureth unto everlasting life, which the Son of man shall give unto you" (John 6:27). Does this language imply that the obtaining of eternal life is a simple matter? It does not; far from it. It denotes that a man must be in deadly earnest, subordinating all other interests in his quest for it, and be prepared to put forth strenuous endeavors and overcome formidable difficulties. Then does this verse teach salvation by works, by self-efforts? No, and yes. No in the sense that anything we do can merit salvation—eternal life is a "gift." Yes in the sense that wholehearted seeking after salvation and a diligent use of the prescribed means of grace are demanded of us. Nowhere in Scripture is there any promise to the dilatory (compare Hebrews 4:11).

"No man can come to me, except the Father which hath sent Me draw him" (John 6:44). Plainly this language exposes the lie of the popular theory of the day, that it lies within the power of man's will to be saved any time he chooses to be. This verse contradicts the flesh-pleasing and creature-honoring idea that anyone can receive Christ as his Savior the moment he decides to do so. The reason why the natural man cannot come to Christ till the Father draws him is because he is the bond-slave of sin (John 8:34), serving divers lusts (Titus 3:3), the captive of the devil (2 Timothy 2:26). Almighty power must break his chains and open the prison doors (Luke 4:18) ere he can come to Christ. Can one who loves darkness and hates the light reverse the process? No, no more than a man who has a diseased foot or poisoned hand can heal it by an effort of will. Can the Ethiopian change his skin or the leopard his spots? No more can they do good who are accustomed to do evil (Jeremiah 13:23).

"And if the righteous scarcely be saved, where shall the ungodly and sinner appear?" (1 Peter 4:18). Matthew Henry said, "It is as much as the best can do to secure the salvation of their souls; there are so many sufferings, temptations, and difficulties to be overcome; so many sins to be mortified; the gate is so strait, and the way so narrow, that it is as much as the righteous man can do to be saved. Let the absolute necessity of salvation balance the difficulty of it. Consider your difficulties are the greatest at first: God offers His grace and help; the contest will not last long. Be but faithful to the death and God will give you the crown of life (Revelation 2:10)."

So also said John Lillie, "After all that God has done by sending His Son, and the Son by the Holy Spirit, it is only with difficulty, exceeding difficulty, that the work of saving the righteous advances to its consummation. The entrance into the kingdom lies through much tribulation—through fightings without and fears within—through the world's seductions and its frowns—through the utter weakness and continual failures of the flesh, and the many fiery darts of Satan."

Here then are the reasons why saving faith is so difficult to put forth:

(1) By nature men are entirely ignorant of its real character, and therefore are easily deceived by Satan's plausible substitutes for it. But even when they are scripturally informed thereon, they either sorrowfully turn their backs on Christ, as did the

rich young ruler when he learned His terms of discipleship, or they hypocritically profess what they do not possess.

(2) The power of self-love reigns supreme within, and to deny self is too great a demand upon the unregenerate.

(3) The love of the world and the approbation of their friends stands in the way of a complete surrender to Christ.

(4) The demands of God that He should be loved with all the heart, and that we should be "holy in all manner of conversation," (1 Peter 1:15) repels the carnal.

(5) Bearing the reproach of Christ, being hated by the religious world (John 15:18), suffering persecution for righteousness' sake, is something that mere flesh and blood shrinks from.

(6) The humbling of ourselves before God, penitently confessing all our self-will, is something which an unbroken heart revolts against.

(7) To fight the good fight of faith (1 Timothy 6:12) and overcome the devil (1 John 2:13) is too arduous an undertaking for those who love their own ease.

Multitudes desire to be saved from hell (the natural instinct of self-preservation) who are quite unwilling to be saved from sin. Yes, there are tens of thousands who have been deluded into thinking that they have "accepted Christ as their Savior," whose lives show plainly that they reject Him as their Lord. For a sinner to obtain the pardon of God he must "forsake his way" (Isaiah 55:7). No man can turn to God until he turns from idols (1 Thessalonians 1:9). Thus insisted the Lord Jesus, "Whosoever he be of you that forsaketh not all that he hath, he cannot be My disciple" (Luke 14:33).

The terrible thing is that so many preachers today, under the pretence of magnifying the grace of God, have represented Christ as the Minister of sin; as One who has, through His atoning sacrifice, procured an indulgence for men to continue grati-

fying their fleshly and worldly lusts. Provided a man professes to
believe in the virgin birth and vicarious death of Christ, and
claims to be resting upon Him alone for salvation, he may pass
for a real Christian almost anywhere today, even though his
daily life may be no different from that of the moral worldling
who makes no profession at all. The devil is chloroforming
thousands into hell by this very delusion. The Lord Jesus asks,
"Why call ye Me, Lord, Lord, and do not the things which I
say?" (Luke 6:46), and insists, "Not every one that saith unto
Me, 'Lord, Lord,' shall enter into the kingdom of heaven; but he
that doeth the will of My Father which is in heaven" (Matthew
7:21).

The hardest task before most of us is not to learn, but to un-
learn. Many of God's own children have drunk so deeply of the
sweetened poison of Satan that it is by no means easy to get it
out of their systems; and while it remains in them it stupefies
their understanding. So much is this the case that the first time
one of them reads an article like this it is apt to strike him as an
open attack upon the sufficiency of Christ's finished work, as
though I were here teaching that the atoning sacrifice of the
Lamb needed to be augmented by something from the creature.
Not so. Nothing but the merits of Immanuel can ever give any
sinner title to stand before the ineffably holy God. But what I
are now contending for is this: When does God impute to any
sinner the righteousness of Christ? Certainly not while he is opposed to Him.

Moreover, we do not honor the work of Christ until we cor-
rectly define what that work was designed to effect. The Lord of
glory did not come here and die to procure the pardon of our
sins, and take us to heaven while our hearts still remain cleaving
to the earth. No, He came here to prepare a way to heaven (John
10:4; 14:2-3; Hebrews 10:20-22; 1 Peter 2:21), to call men into

that way that by His precepts and promises, His example and spirit, He might form and fashion their souls to that glorious state, and make them willing to abandon all things for it. He lived and died so that His Spirit would come and quicken the dead sinners into newness of life, make them new creatures in Himself, and cause them to sojourn in this world as those who are not of it, as those whose hearts have already departed from it. Christ did not come here to render a change of heart, repentance, faith, personal holiness, loving God supremely, and obeying Him unreservedly, as unnecessary, or salvation as possible without them. How strange it is that any suppose He did!

Ah, my reader, it becomes a searching test for each of our hearts to face honestly the question, Is this what I really long for? As Bunyan asked (in his *The Jerusalem Sinner Saved*), "What are thy desires? Wouldest thou be saved? Wouldest thou be saved with a thorough salvation? Wouldest thou be saved from guilt, and from filth too? Wouldest thou be the servant of the Savior? Art thou indeed weary of the service of thy old masters, the devil, sin, and the world? And have these desires put thy soul to flight? Dost thou fly to Him that is a Savior from the wrath to come, for life? If these be thy desires, and if they be unfeigned, fear not."

Charles Spurgeon, in a sermon on Matthew 9:12, said, "Many people think that when we preach salvation, we mean salvation from going to hell. We do mean that, but we mean a great deal more: we preach salvation from sin; we say that Christ is able to save a man; and we mean by that that He is able to save him from sin and to make him holy, to make him a new man. No person has any right to say 'I am saved,' while he continues in sin as he did before. How can you be saved from sin while you are living in it? A man who is drowning cannot say he is saved from the water while he is sinking in it; a man who is frost-bitten cannot say with any truth that he is saved from the cold while he is stiffened in the wintry blast. No, man, Christ did not come to save you in your sins, but to save you from your sins; not to make the disease so that it should not kill you, but to let it remain in itself mortal, and, nevertheless, to remove it from you, and you from it. Christ Jesus came then to heal us from the plague of sin, to touch us with His hand and say 'I will, be thou clean.' "

They who do not yearn after holiness of heart and righteousness of life are only deceiving themselves when they suppose they desire to be saved by Christ. The plain fact is, all that is wanted by so many today is merely a soothing portion of their conscience, which will enable them to go on comfortably in a course of self-pleasing which will permit them to continue their worldly ways without the fear of eternal punishment. Human nature is the same the world over; that wretched instinct which causes multitudes to believe that paying a papist priest a few dollars procures forgiveness of all their past sins, and an "indulgence" for future ones moves other multitudes to devour greedily the lie that, with an unbroken and impenitent heart, by a mere act of the will, they may "believe in Christ," and thereby obtain not only God's pardon for past sins, but an "eternal security," no matter what they do or do not do in the future.

Oh, my reader, do not be deceived. God frees none from the condemnation but those who are in Christ Jesus; and "if any man be in Christ, he is a new creature: old things are [not "ought to be"] passed away; behold, all things are become new (2 Corinthians 5:17). Saving faith makes a sinner come to Christ with a real soul-thirst so that he may drink of the living water, even of His sanctifying Spirit (John 7:38-39). To love our enemies, to bless them who curse us, to pray for them who despitefully use us, is very far from being easy; yet this is only one part of the task that Christ assigns unto those who would be His disciples. He acted thus, and He has left us an example that we should follow His steps. And His "salvation," in its present application, consists of revealing to our hearts the imperative need for our measuring up to His high and holy standard, with a realization of our own utter powerlessness so to do, and creating within us an intense hunger and thirst after such personal righteousness, and a daily turning unto Him and trustful supplication for needed grace and strength.

6

Saving Faith:
Its Communication

From the human viewpoint, things are now in a bad state in the world. But from the spiritual viewpoint things are in a far worse state in the religious realm. It is sad to see the anti-Christian cults flourishing on every side; but it is far more grievous for those who are taught of God to discover that much of the so-called "gospel" that is now being preached in many "fundamentalist churches" and "gospel halls" is but a satanic delusion. The devil knows that his captives are quite secure while the grace of God and the finished work of Christ are "faithfully" proclaimed to them, so long as the only way in which sinners receive the saving virtues of the atonement is unfaithfully concealed. While God's peremptory and unchanging demand for repentance is left out, while Christ's own terms of discipleship (i.e., how to become a Christian, Acts 11:26) in Luke 14:26, 27, 33 are withheld, and while saving faith is frittered down to a mere act of the will, blind laymen will continue to be led by blind preachers, only for both to fall into the ditch.

Things are far, far worse even in the "orthodox" sections of Christendom than the majority of God's own children are aware. Things are rotten even at the very foundation, for with very rare exceptions God's way of salvation is no longer being taught. Tens of thousands are ever learning points in prophecy, the meaning of the types, the significance of the numerals, how to divide the "dispensations," who are, nevertheless, never able to come to the knowledge of the truth (2 Timothy 3:7) of salvation itself—unable because unwilling to pay the price (Proverbs 23:23), which is a full surrender to God Himself. As far as this writer understands the present situation, it seems to him that what is needed today is to press upon the serious attention of professing Christians such questions as: When is it that God applies to a sinner the virtues of Christ's finished work? What is it that I am called upon to do in order to appropriate myself to the efficacy of Christ's atonement? What is it that gives me an actual entrance into the good of His redemption?

The questions formulated above are only three different ways of framing the same inquiry. Now the popular answer that is being returned to them is, "Nothing more is required from any sinner than that he simply believe on the Lord Jesus Christ." In the preceding articles of this series I have sought to show that such a reply is misleading, inadequate, faulty, and that because it ignores all the other scriptures that set forth what God requires from the sinner. It leaves out of account God's demand for repentance (with all that that involves and includes), and Christ's clearly defined terms of discipleship in Luke 14. To restrict ourselves to any one scripture term of a subject, or set of passages using that term, results in an erroneous conception of it. They who limit their ideas of regeneration to the one figure of the new birth lapse into serious error upon it. So they who limit their thoughts on how to be saved to the one word "believe" are easily misled. Diligent care needs to be taken to collect all that Scripture teaches on any subject if we are to have a properly balanced and accurate view thereof.

Let me be more specific. In Romans 10:13 we read: "For whosoever shall call upon the name of the Lord shall be saved."

Now does this mean that all who have, with their lips, cried
unto the Lord, who have in the name of Christ sought God to
have mercy on them, have been saved by Him? They who reply
in the affirmative are only deceived by the mere sound of words,
as the deluded Romanist is when he contends for Christ's bodily presence in the bread because He said, "This is My body."
And how are we to show the papist that he is misled? Why, by
comparing Scripture with Scripture. So it is here. The writer
well remembers being on a ship in a terrible storm off the coast
of Newfoundland. All the hatches were battened down, and for
three days no passenger was allowed on the decks. Reports from
the stewards were disquieting. Strong men paled. As the winds
increased and the ship rolled worse and worse, scores of men
and women were heard calling upon the name of the Lord. Did
He save them? A day or two later, when the weather changed,
those same men and women were drinking, cursing, and card-
playing!

Perhaps someone asks, "But does not Romans 10:13 say
what it means?" Certainly it does, but no verse of Scripture
yields its meaning to lazy people. Christ Himself tells us that
there are many who call Him "Lord" to whom He will say, "Depart from Me" (Matthew 7:22-23). Then what is to be done
with Romans 10:13? Why, diligently compare it with all other
passages that make known what the sinner must do ere God will
save him. If nothing more than the fear of death or horror of
hell prompts the sinner to call upon the Lord, he might just as
well call upon the trees. The Almighty is not at the beck and call
of any rebel who, when he is terrified, sues for mercy. "He that
turneth away his ear from hearing the law, even his prayer shall
be abomination" (Proverbs 28:9)! "He that covereth his sins
shall not prosper; but whoso confesseth and forsaketh them
shall have mercy" (Proverbs 28: 13). The only "calling upon His

name" that the Lord heeds is that which issues from a broken, penitent, sin-hating heart that thirsts after holiness.

The same principle applies to Acts 16:31, and all similar texts: "Believe on the Lord Jesus Christ, and thou shalt be saved." To a casual reader, that seems a very simple matter, yet a closer pondering of those words should discover that more is involved than at first sight appears. Note that the apostles did not merely tell the Philippian jailer to "rest on the finished work of Christ," or "trust in His atoning sacrifice." Instead, it was a Person who was set before him. Again, it was not simply "Believe on the Savior," but "the Lord Jesus Christ." John 1:12 shows plainly that to "believe" is to "receive," and to be saved a sinner must receive One who is not only Savior, but "Lord," yea, who must be received as "Lord" before He becomes the Savior of that person. And to receive "Christ Jesus the Lord" (Colossians 2:6) necessarily involves the renouncing of our own sinful lordship, the throwing down of the weapons of our warfare against Him, and the submitting to His yoke and rule. And before any human rebel is brought to do that, a miracle of divine grace has to be wrought within him. And this brings us more immediately to the present aspect of our theme.

Saving faith is not a native product of the human heart, but a spiritual grace communicated from on high. "It is the gift of God" (Ephesians 2:8). It is "of the operation of God" (Colossians 2:12). It is by "the power of God" (1 Corinthians 2:5). A most remarkable passage on this subject is found in Ephesians 1:16-20. There we find the Apostle Paul praying that the saints should have the eyes of their understanding enlightened, that they might know "what is the exceeding greatness of His power to us-ward who believe, according to the working of His mighty power, which He wrought in Christ when He raised Him from the dead." Not the strong power of God, or the greatness of it, but the "exceeding greatness of His power to usward." Note too the standard of comparison: we "believe according to the working of His mighty power, which He wrought in Christ when He raised Him from the dead."

God put forth His Mighty power when He resurrected Christ. There was a mighty power seeking to hinder, even Satan and all his hosts. There was a mighty difficulty to be overcome, even the vanquishing of the grace. There was a mighty result to be achieved, even the bringing to life of One who was dead. None but God Himself was equal to a miracle so stupendous. Strictly analogous is that miracle of grace that issues in saving faith. The devil employs all his arts and power to retain his captive. The sinner is dead in trespasses and sins, and can no more quicken himself than he can create a world. His heart is bound fast with the grave clothes of worldly and fleshly lusts, and only Omnipotence can raise it into communion with God. Well may every true servant of the Lord emulate the Apostle Paul and pray earnestly that God will enlighten His people concerning this wonder of wonders, so that, instead of attributing their faith to an exercise of their own will, they may freely ascribe all the honor and glory unto Him to whom alone it justly belongs.

If only the professing Christians of this untoward generation could begin to obtain some adequate conception of the real condition of every man by nature, they might be less inclined to cavil against the teaching that nothing short of a miracle of grace can ever qualify any sinner to believe unto the saving of his soul. If they could only see that the heart's attitude towards God of the most refined and moral is not a whit different from that of the most vulgar and vicious; that he who is most kind and benevolent toward his fellow creatures has no more real desire after Christ than has the most selfish and brutal; then it would be evident that divine power must operate to change the heart. Divine power was needed to create, but much greater power is required to regenerate a soul. Creation is only the bringing of something out of nothing; but regeneration is the transforming not only of an unlovely object, but of one that resists with all its might the gracious designs of the heavenly Potter.

It is not simply that the Holy Spirit approaches a heart in which there is no love for God, but He finds it filled with enmity against Him, and incapable of being subject to His law (Romans 8:7). True, the individual himself may be quite unconscious of this terrible fact, yea, ready indignantly to deny it. But that is easily accounted for. If he has heard little or nothing but the love, the grace, the mercy, the goodness of God, it would indeed be surprising if he hated Him. But once the God of Scripture is made known to him in the power of the Spirit, once he is made to realize that God is the Governor of this world, demanding unqualified submission to all His laws; that He is inflexibly just, and "will by no means clear the guilty"; that He is sovereign, and loves whom He pleases and hates whom He wills; that so far from being an easy-going, indulgent Creator who winks at the follies of His creatures, He is ineffably holy, so that His righteous wrath burns against all the workers of iniquity— then will people be conscious of indwelling enmity surging up against Him. And nothing but the almighty power of the Spirit can overcome that enmity and bring any rebel truly to love the God of Holy Writ.

Rightly did Thomas Goodwin the Puritan say, "A wolf will sooner marry a lamb, or a lamb a wolf, than ever a carnal heart be subject to the law of God, which was the ancient husband of it (Romans 7:6). It is the turning of one contrary into another. To turn water into wine, there is some kind of symbolizing, yet that is a miracle. But to turn a wolf into a lamb, to turn fire into

water, is a yet greater miracle. Between nothing and something
there is an infinite distance, but between sin and grace there is a
greater distance than can be between nothing and the highest
angel in heaven. . . .To destroy the power of sin in a man's soul
is as great a work as to take away the guilt of sin. It is easier to
say to a blind man, 'See,' and to a lame man, 'Walk,' than to say
to a man who lies under the power of sin, 'Live, be holy,' for
there is that that will not be subject."

In 2 Corinthians 10:4-5, the apostle describes the character
of that work in which the true servants of Christ are engaged. It
is a conflict with the forces of Satan. The weapons of their warfare are "not carnal"—as well might modern soldiers go forth
equipped with only wooden swords and paper shields as preachers think to liberate the devil's captives by means of human
leaning, worldly methods, touching anecdotes, attractive singing, and so on. No, their weapons are the Word of God and all
prayer (Ephesians 6:17-18); and even these are only mighty
"through God," that is by His direct and special blessing of
them to particular souls. In what follows, a description is given
of where the might of God is seen, namely in the powerful opposition that it meets with and vanquishes, "to the pulling down
of strong holds, casting down imaginations, and every high
thing that exalteth itself against the knowledge of God, and
bringing into captivity every thought to the obedience of
Christ."

Herein lies the power of God when He is pleased thus to
put it forth in the saving of a sinner. The heart of that sinner is
fortified against Him; it is steeled against His holy demands, His
righteous claims. It is determined not to submit to His law, nor
to abandon those idols that it prohibits. That haughty rebel has
made up his mind that he will not turn away from the delights
of this world and the pleasure of sin and give God the supreme

place in his affections. But God has determined to overcome his sinful opposition, and transform him into a loving and loyal subject. The figure here used is that of a besieged town—the heart. Its "strongholds"—the reigning power of fleshly and worldly lusts—are pulled down; self-will is broken, pride is subdued, and the defiant rebel is made a willing captive to "the obedience of Christ"! "Mighty through God" points to this miracle of grace.

There is one other detail pointed to by the analogy drawn in Ephesians 1:19-20, that exemplifies the mighty power of God, namely "and set Him [Christ] at His own right hand in the heavenly places." The members of Christ's mystical body are predestined to be conformed to the glorious image of their glorified Head—in measure, now; perfectly, in the day to come. The ascension of Christ was contrary to nature, being opposed by the law of gravitation. But the power of God overcame that opposition, and translated His resurrected Son bodily into heaven. In like manner, His grace produces in His people that which is contrary to nature, overcoming the opposition of the flesh, and drawing their hearts unto things above. How we would marvel if we saw a man extend his arms and suddenly leave the earth, soaring upward into the sky. Yet still more wonderful is it when we behold the power of the Spirit causing a sinful creature to rise above temptations, worldliness and sin, and breathe the atmosphere of heaven; when a human soul is made to disdain the things of earth and find its satisfaction in things above.

The historical order in connection with the Head in Ephesians 1:19-20, is also the experimental order with regard to the members of His body. Before setting His Son at His own right hand in the heavenlies, God raised Him from the dead; so before the Holy Spirit fixes the heart of a sinner upon Christ He first quickens him into newness of life. There must be life before there can be sight, believing, or good works performed. One who is physically dead is incapable of doing anything; so he who is spiritually dead is incapable of any spiritual exercises. First the giving of life unto dead Lazarus, then the removing of the grave-clothes that bound him hand and foot. God must regenerate before there can be a "new creature in Christ Jesus." The washing of a child follows its birth.

When spiritual life has been communicated to the soul, that individual is now able to see things in their true colors. In God's light he sees light (Psalm 36:9). He is now given to perceive (by the Holy Spirit) what a lifelong rebel he has been against his Creator and Benefactor; that instead of making God's will his rule, he has gone his own way; that instead of having before him God's glory he has sought only to please and gratify self. Even though he may have been preserved from all the grosser outward forms of wickedness, he now recognizes that he is a spiritual leper, a vile and polluted creature, utterly unfit to draw near, still less to dwell with Him who is ineffably holy; and such an apprehension makes him feel that his case is hopeless.

There is a vast difference between hearing or reading of what conviction of sin is and being made to feel it in the depths of one's own soul. Multitudes are acquainted with the theory who are total strangers to the experience of it. One may read of the sad effects of war, and may agree that they are indeed dreadful; but when the enemy is at one's own door, plundering his goods, firing his home, and slaying his dear ones, he is far more sensible of the miseries of war than ever he was (or could be) previously. So an unbeliever may hear of what a dreadful state the sinner is in before God, and how terrible will be the sufferings of hell; but when the Spirit brings home to his own heart its actual condition, and makes him feel the heat of God's wrath in his own conscience, he is ready to sink with dismay and despair. Reader, do you know anything of such an experience?

Only thus is any soul prepared truly to appreciate Christ. They who are whole do not need a physician. The one who has been savingly convicted is made to realize that none but the Lord Jesus can heal one so desperately diseased by sin; that He alone can impart that spiritual health (holiness) which will enable him to run in the way of God's commandments; that nothing but His precious blood can atone for the sins of the past, and naught but His all-sufficient grace can meet the pressing needs of the present and future. Thus there must be discerning faith before there is coming faith. The Father draws to the Son (John 6:44) by imparting to the mind a deep realization of our desperate need of Christ, by giving to the heart a real sense of the inestimable worth of Him, and by causing the will to receive Him on His own terms.

7

Saving Faith: Its Evidences

The great majority of those who read this will, doubtless, be they who profess to be in possession of a saving faith. To all such I would put these questions: Where is your proof? What effects has it produced in you? A tree is known by its fruits, and a fountain by the waters that issue from it; so the nature of your faith may be ascertained by a careful examination of what it is bringing forth. I say "a careful examination," for as all fruit is not fit for eating, nor all water for drinking, so all works are not the effects of a faith that saves. Reformation is not regeneration, and a changed life does not always indicate a changed heart. Have you been saved from a dislike of God's commandments and a disrelish of His holiness? Have you been saved from pride, covetousness, and murmuring? Have you been delivered from the love of this world, from the fear of man, and from the reigning power of every sin?

The heart of fallen man is thoroughly depraved, its thoughts and imaginations being only evil continually (Genesis 6:5). It is full of corrupt desires and affections, that exert themselves and influence man in all he does. Now the gospel comes into direct opposition with these selfish lusts and corrupt affections, both in the root and in the fruit of them (Titus 2:11-12). There is no greater duty that the gospel urges upon our souls than the mortifying and destroying of them, and this indispensably, if we intend to be made partakers of its promises (Romans 8:13; Colossians 3:5, 8). Hence the first real work of faith is to cleanse the soul from these pollutions, and therefore we read: "They that are Christ's have crucified the flesh with the affections and lusts" (Galatians 5:24). Mark well, it is not that they "ought to" do so, but that they have actually done so, in some measure or degree.

It is one thing really to think we believe a thing, it is quite another actually to do so. So fickle is the human heart that even in natural things men do not know their own minds. In temporal affairs what a man really believes is best ascertained by his practice. Suppose I meet a traveler in a narrow gorge and tell him that just ahead is an impassable river, and that the bridge across it is rotten. If he declines to turn back, am I not warranted in concluding that he does not believe me? Or if a physician tells me a certain disease holds me in its grip, and that in a short time it will prove fatal if I do not use a prescribed remedy that is sure to heal, would he not be justified in inferring that I did not trust his judgment were he to see me not only ignoring his directions but following a contrary course? Likewise, to believe there is a hell and yet run unto it, to believe that sin continued in will damn and yet live in it—to what purpose is it to boast of such a faith?

Now, from what was before us in the above section, it should be plain beyond all room for doubt that, when God imparts saving faith to a soul, radical and real effects will follow. One cannot be raised from the dead without there being a consequent walking in newness of life. One cannot be the subject of a miracle of grace being wrought in the heart without a noticeable change being apparent to all who know him. Where a supernatural root has been implanted, supernatural fruit must issue therefrom. Not that sinless perfection is attained in this life, nor that the evil principle, the flesh, is eradicated from our be-

ings, or even purified. Nevertheless, there is now a yearning after perfection; there is a spirit resisting the flesh; there is a striving against sin. And more, there is a growing in grace, and a
pressing forward along the "narrow way" that leads to heaven.

One serious error so widely propagated today in "orthodox"
circles, and that is responsible for so many souls being deceived,
is the seemingly Christ-honoring doctrine that it is "His blood
which alone saves any sinner." Ah, Satan is very clever; he
knows exactly what bait to use for every place in which he fishes.
Many a company would indignantly resent a preacher's telling
them that getting baptized and eating the Lord's supper were
God's appointed means for saving the soul; yet most of these
same people will readily accept the lie that it is only by the blood
of Christ we can be saved. That is true Godwards, but it is not
true manwards. The work of the Spirit in us is equally essential
as the work of Christ for us. Let the reader carefully ponder the
whole of Titus 3:5.

Salvation is twofold: it is both legal and experimental, and
consists of justification and sanctification. Moreover, I owe my
salvation not only to the Son, but to all three persons in the
Godhead. Alas, how little this is realized today, and how little it
is preached. First, and primarily, I owe my salvation to God the
Father, who ordained and planned it, and who chose me unto
salvation (2 Thessalonians 2:13). In Titus 3:4, it is the Father
who is denominated "God our Savior." Second, and meritori-
ously, I owe my salvation to the obedience and sacrifice of God
the Son Incarnate, who performed as my Sponsor everything
that the law required, and satisfied all its demands upon me.
Third, and efficaciously, I owe my salvation to the regenerating,
sanctifying, and preserving operations of the Spirit. Note that
His work is made just as prominent in Luke 15:8-10 as is the
Shepherd's in Luke 15:4-7! As Titus 3:5 so plainly affirms, God

"saved us by the washing of regeneration and renewing of the Holy Ghost"; and it is the presence of His fruit in my heart and life that furnishes the immediate evidence of my salvation.

"With the heart man believeth unto righteousness" (Romans 10:10). Thus it is the heart that we must first examine in order to discover evidences of the presence of a saving faith. And first, God's Word speaks of "purifying their hearts by faith" (Acts 15:9). Of old the Lord said, "O Jerusalem, wash thine heart from wickedness, that thou mayest be saved" (Jeremiah 4:14). A heart that is being purified by faith (cf. 1 Peter 1:22) is one fixed upon a pure Object. It drinks from a pure Fountain, delights in a pure Law (Romans 7:22), and looks forward to spending eternity with a pure Savior (1 John 3:3). It loathes all that is filthy—spiritually as well as morally—yea, hates the very garment spotted by the flesh (Jude 23). Contrariwise, it loves all that is holy, lovely and Christ-like.

"The pure in heart shall see God" (Matthew 5:8). Heart purity is absolutely essential to fit us for dwelling in that place into which there shall in no wise enter anything "that defileth, neither whatsoever worketh abomination" (Revelation 21:27). Perhaps a little fuller definition is called for. Purifying the heart by faith consists of, first, the purifying of the understanding by the shining in of divine light, so as to cleanse it from error. It consists, second, in the purifying of the conscience, so as to cleanse it from guilt. Third, it consists in the purifying of the will, so as to cleanse it from self-will and self-seeking. Fourth, it consists in the purifying of the affections, so as to cleanse them from the love of all that is evil. In Scripture the "heart" includes all these four faculties. A deliberate purpose to continue in any one sin cannot consist with a pure heart.

Again, saving faith is always evidenced by a humble heart. Faith lays the soul low, for it discovers its own vileness, empti-

ness, and impotence. It realizes its former sinfulness and present
unworthiness. It is conscious of its weaknesses and wants, its
carnality and corruptions. Nothing more exalts Christ than
faith, and nothing more debases a man. In order to magnify the
riches of His grace, God has selected faith as the fittest instru-
ment, and this because it is that which causes us to go entirely
out from ourselves unto Him. Faith, realizing we are nothing
but sin and wretchedness, comes unto Christ as an empty-
handed beggar to receive all from Him. Faith empties a man of
self-conceit, self-confidence, and self-righteousness, and makes
him seem to be nothing so that Christ may be all in all. The
strongest faith is always accompanied by the greatest humility,
accounting self the greatest of sinners and unworthy of the least
favor (see Matthew 8:8-10).

Again, saving faith is always found in a tender heart. "A new
heart also will I give you, and a new spirit will I put within you;
and I will take away the stony heart out of your flesh, and I will
give you an heart of flesh" (Ezekiel 36:26). An unregenerate
heart is hard as stone, full of pride and presumption. It is quite
unmoved by the sufferings of Christ, in the sense that they act
as no deterrent against self-will and self-pleasing. But the real
Christian is moved by the love of Christ, and says, "How can I
sin against His dying love for me." When overtaken by a fault,
there is passionate relenting and bitter mourning. Oh, my
reader, do you know what it is to be melted before God, for you
to be heart-broken with anguish over sinning against and grieving such a Savior? Ah, it is not the absence of sin, but the grieving over it that distinguishes the child of God from empty professors.

Another characteristic of saving faith is that it "worketh by
love" (Galatians 5:6). It is not inactive, but energetic. That faith
which is "of the operation of God" (Colossians 2:12) is a mighty

principle of power, diffusing spiritual energy to all the faculties
of the soul and enlisting them in the service of God. Faith is a
principle of life by which the Christian lives unto God; a principle of motion by which he walks to heaven along the highway of
holiness; a principle of strength by which he opposes the flesh,
the world, and the devil. "Faith in the heart of a Christian is like
the salt that was thrown into the corrupt fountain, that made
the naughty waters good and the barren land fruitful. Hence it
is that there followeth an alteration of life and conversation,
and so bringeth forth fruit accordingly. 'A good man out of the
good treasure of the heart bringeth forth good fruit,' which
treasure is faith" (John Bunyan in *Christian Behavior*).

Where a saving faith is rooted in the heart, it grows up and
spreads itself in all the branches of obedience, and is filled with
the fruits of righteousness. It makes its possessor act for God,
and thereby evidences that it is a living thing and not merely a
lifeless theory. Even a newborn infant, though it cannot walk
and work as a grown man, breathes and cries, moves and sucks,
and thereby shows it is alive. So it is with the one who has been
born again: there is a breathing unto God, a crying after Him, a
moving toward Him, a clinging to Him. But the infant does not
long remain a babe; there is growth, increasing strength, en-
larged activity. Nor does the Christian remain stationary. He
goes "from strength to strength" (Psalm 84:7).

But observe carefully, faith not only "worketh" but it
"worketh by love." It is at this point that the works of the Christian differ from those of the mere religionist. "The papist works
that he may merit heaven. The Pharisee works that he may be
applauded, that he may be seen of men, that he may have a
good esteem with them. The slave works lest he should be
beaten, lest he should be damned. The formalist works that he
may stop the mouth of conscience, that will be accusing him if

he does nothing. The ordinary professor works because it is a shame to do nothing where so much is professed. But the true believer works because he loves. This is the principal, if not the only, motive that sets him a-work. If there were no other motive within or without him, yet would he be working for God, acting for Christ, because he loves Him; it is like fire in his bones" (David Clarkson).

Saving faith is ever accompanied by an obedient walk. "Hereby we do know that we know Him, if we keep His commandments. He that saith, 'I know Him,' and keepeth not His commandments, is a liar, and the truth is not in him" (1 John 2:3-4). Make no mistake upon this point: infinite as are the merits of Christ's sacrifice, mighty as is the potency of His priestly intercession, yet they do not avail for any who continue in the path of disobedience. He acknowledges none to be His disciples save them who do homage to Him as their Lord. "Too many professors pacify themselves with the idea that they possess imputed righteousness while they are indifferent to the sanctifying work of the Spirit. They refuse to put on the garment of obedience; they reject the white linen, which is the righteousness of the saints. They thus reveal their self-will, their enmity to God, and their non-submission to His Son. Such men may talk what they will about justification by faith and salvation by grace, but they are rebels at heart; they have nothing more on the wedding dress than the self-righteous, whom they so eagerly condemn. The fact is, if we wish for the blessings of grace, we must in our hearts submit to the rules of grace without picking and choosing" (C. H. Spurgeon on "The Wedding Garment").

Once more, saving faith is precious, for, like gold, it will endure trial (1 Peter 1:7). A genuine Christian fears no test; he is willing, yea, wishes, to be tried by God Himself. He cries, "Examine me, O Lord, and prove me; try my reins and my heart"

(Psalm 26:2). Therefore he is willing for his faith to be tried by others, for he does not shun the touchstone of Holy Writ. He frequently tries for himself, for where so much is at stake he must be sure. He is anxious to know the worst as well as the best. That preaching pleases him best that is most searching and discriminating. He is loath to be deluded with vain hopes. He would not be flattered into a high conceit of his spiritual state without grounds. When challenged, he complies with the apostle's advice in 2 Corinthians 13:5.

Herein the real Christian differs from the formalist. The presumptuous professor is filled with pride, and, having a high opinion of himself, is quite sure that he has been saved by Christ. He disdains any searching tests, and considers self-examination to be highly injurious and destructive of faith. That preaching pleases him best which keeps at a respectable distance, which does not come near his conscience, which makes no scrutiny of his heart. To preach to him of the finished work of Christ and the eternal security of all who believe in Him strengthens his false peace and feeds his carnal confidence. Should a real servant of God seek to convince him that his hope is a delusion, and his confidence presumptuous, he would regard him as an enemy, as Satan seeking to fill him with doubts. There is more hope of a murderer being saved than of his being disillusioned.

Another characteristic of saving faith is that it gives the heart victory over all the vanities and vexations of things below. "For whatsoever is born of God overcometh the world; and this is the victory that overcometh the world, even our faith" (1 John 5:4). Observe that this is not an ideal after which the Christian strives, but an actuality of present experience. In this the saint is conformed to His Head. "Be of good cheer, I have overcome the world" (John 16:33). Christ overcame it *for* His people, and now

He overcomes it *in* them. He opens their eyes to see the hollow-
ness and worthlessness of the best that this world has to offer,
and weans their hearts from it by satisfying them with spiritual
things. So little does the world attract the genuine child of God
that he longs for the time to come when God shall take him out
of it.

Alas, that so very few of those now bearing the name of
Christ have any real experimental acquaintance with these
things. Alas, that so many are deceived by a faith that is not a
saving one. "He only is a Christian who lives for Christ. Many
persons think they can be Christians on easier terms than these.
They think it is enough to trust in Christ while they do not live
for Him. But the Bible teaches us that if we are partakers of
Christ's death, we are also partakers of His life. If we have any
such appreciation of His love in dying for us as to lead us to
confide in the merits of His death, we shall be constrained to
consecrate our lives to His service. And this is the only evidence
of the genuineness of our faith" (Charles Hodge on 2 Corinthians 5:15).

Reader, are the things mentioned above actualized in your
own experience? If they are not, how worthless and wicked is
your profession! "It is therefore exceedingly absurd for any to
pretend that they have a good heart while they live a wicked life,
or do not bring forth the fruit of universal holiness in their
practice. Men who live in the ways of sin, and yet flatter themselves that they shall go to heaven, expecting to be received
hereafter as holy persons, without a holy practice, act as though
they expected to make a fool of their Judge. This is implied in
what the apostle says (speaking of men's doing good works and
living a holy life, thereby exhibiting evidence of their title to everlasting life), 'Be not deceived. God is not mocked; for whatsoever a man soweth, that shall he also reap' (Galatians 6:7). This

is as much as to say, Do not deceive yourselves with an expectation of reaping life everlasting hereafter, if you do not sow to the Spirit here; it is in vain to think that God will be made a fool of by you" (Jonathan Edwards in *Religious Affections*).

That which Christ requires from His disciples is that they should magnify and glorify Him in this world, and that by living holily to Him and suffering patiently for Him. Nothing is as honoring to Christ as that those who bear His name should, by their holy obedience, make manifest the power of His love over their hearts and lives. Contrariwise, nothing is so great a reproach to Him, nothing more dishonors Him, than that those who are living to please self, and who are conformed to this world, should cloak their wickedness under His holy name. A Christian is one who has taken Christ for his example in all things. Then how great the insult that is done Him by those claiming to be Christians whose daily lives show they have no respect for His godly example. They are a stench in His nostrils; they are a cause of grievous sorrow to His real disciples; they are the greatest hindrance of all to the progress of His cause on earth; and they shall yet find that the hottest places in hell have been reserved for them. Oh, that they would either abandon their course of self-pleasing or drop the profession of that name which is above every name.

Should the Lord be pleased to use this article in shattering the false confidence of some deluded souls, and should they earnestly inquire how they are to obtain a genuine and saving faith, I answer, use the means that God has prescribed. When faith is His gift, He gives it in His own way; and if we desire to receive it, then we must put ourselves in that way wherein He is wont to communicate it. Faith is the work of God, but He does not work it immediately, but through the channels of His appointed means. The means prescribed cannot effect faith of themselves. They are no further effectual than in instruments in the hands of Him who is the principal cause. Though He has not tied Himself to them, yet He has confined us. Though He is free, yet the means are necessary to us.

The first means is prayer. "A new heart also will I give you, and a new spirit will I put within you" (Ezekiel 36:26). Here is a gracious promise, but in what way will He accomplish it, and similar ones? Listen, "Thus saith the Lord God; I will yet for this be enquired of by the house of Israel, to do it for them'" (Ezekiel 36:37). Cry earnestly to God for a new heart, for His regenerating Spirit, for the gift of saving faith. Prayer is a universal duty. Though an unbeliever sins in praying (as in everything else), it is not a sin for him to pray.

The second means is the written Word heard (John 17:20; 1 Corinthians 3:5) or read (2 Timothy 3:15). Said David, "I will never forget Thy precepts, for with them Thou hast quickened me" (Psalm 119:93). The Scriptures are the Word of God; through them He speaks. Then read them, asking Him to speak life, power, deliverance, and peace to your heart. May the Lord deign to add His blessing.

Part 3

Coming to Christ

8

Coming to Christ

By way of introduction let me bring before the readers the following Scriptures:

1. "Ye will not come to me, that ye might have life" (John 5:40).

2. "Come unto me, all ye that labor and are heavy laden, and I will give you rest" (Matthew 11:28).

3. "No man can come to Me, except the Father which hath sent Me draw him" (John 6:44).

4. "All that the Father giveth Me shall come to Me; and him that cometh to Me I will in no wise cast out" (John 6:37).

5. "If any man come to me, and hate not his father, and mother, and wife, and children, and brethren, and sisters, yea, and his own life also, he cannot be my disciple. And whosoever doth not bear his cross, and come after me, cannot be my disciple" (Luke 14:26-27).

6. "To whom coming, as unto a living stone, disallowed indeed of men, but chosen of God, and precious" (1 Peter 2:4).

7. "Wherefore he is able also to save them to the uttermost that come unto God by him, seeing he ever liveth to make intercession for them" (Hebrews 7:25).

The first of these passages applies to every unregenerate man and woman on this earth. While he is in a state of nature, no man can come to Christ. Though all excellencies, both divine and human, are found in the Lord Jesus, though He is "alto-

gether lovely" (Song of Solomon 5:16), yet the fallen sons of
Adam see in Him no beauty that they should desire Him. They
may be well instructed in the doctrine of Christ, they may believe unhesitatingly all that Scripture affirms concerning Him,
they may frequently take His name upon their lips, profess to be
resting on His finished work, and sing His praises, yet their
hearts are far from Him. The things of this world have the first
place in their affections. Gratifying self is their dominant concern. They do not surrender their lives to Him. He is too holy to
suit their love of sin. His claims are too exacting to suit their
selfish hearts. His terms of discipleship are too severe to suit
their fleshly ways. They will not yield to His Lordship—true alike
with each one of us till God performs a miracle of grace upon
our hearts.

The second of these passages contains a gracious invitation,
made by the compassionate Savior to a particular class of sinners. The "all" is at once qualified, clearly and definitely, by the
words that immediately follow it. The character of those to
whom this loving word belongs is clearly defined: it is those who
"labor" and are "heavy laden." Most clearly then it does not apply to the vast majority of our light-headed, gay-hearted, pleas-
ure-seeking fellows who have no regard for God's glory and no
concern about their eternal welfare. No, the word for such poor
creatures is rather, "Rejoice, O young man, in thy youth; and let
thy heart cheer thee in the days of thy youth, and walk in the
ways of thine heart, and in the sight of thine eyes. But know
thou, that for all these things God will bring thee into judgment" (Ecclesiastes 11:9). But to those who have labored hard to
keep the law and please God, who are "heavy laden" with a felt
sense of their utter inability to meet His requirements, and who
long to be delivered from the power and pollution of sin, Christ
says, "Come unto Me, and I will give you rest."

The third passage quoted above at once tells us that "coming to Christ" is not the easy matter so many imagine it, nor so simple a thing as most preachers represent it to be. Instead of its so being, the incarnate Son of God positively declares that such an act is utterly impossible to a fallen and depraved creature unless and until divine power is brought to bear upon him. A most pride-humbling, flesh-withering, man-abasing word is this. "Coming to Christ" is a far, far different thing from raising your hand to be prayed for by some Protestant "priest," coming forward and taking some cheap-jack evangelist's hand, signing some "decision" card, uniting with some "church," or any other of the "many inventions" (Ecclesiastes 7:29) of man. Before anyone can or will "come to Christ" the understanding must be supernaturally enlightened, the heart must be supernaturally changed, and the stubborn will must be supernaturally broken.

The fourth passage is also one that is unpalatable to the carnal mind, yet is it a precious portion unto the Spirit-taught children of God. It sets forth the blessed truth of unconditional election, or the discriminating grace of God. It speaks of a favored people whom the Father gives to His Son. It declares that every one of that blessed company shall come to Christ. Neither the effects of their fall in Adam, the power of indwelling sin, the hatred and untiring efforts of Satan, nor the deceptive delusions of blind preachers, will be able to finally hinder them. When God's appointed hour arrives, each of His elect is delivered from the power of darkness and is translated into the kingdom of His dear Son. It announces that each such one who comes to Christ, no matter how unworthy and vile he is in himself, no matter how black and long the awful catalogue of his sins, He will by no means despise or fail to welcome him, and under no circumstances will He ever cast him off.

The fifth passage is one that makes known the terms on which alone Christ is willing to receive sinners. Here the uncompromising claims of His holiness are set out. He must be crowned Lord of all, or He will not be Lord at all. There must be the complete heart-renunciation of all that stands in competition with Him. He will tolerate no rival. All that pertains to "the flesh," whether found in a loved one or in self, has to be hated. The "cross" is the badge of Christian discipleship—not a golden one worn on the body, but the principle of self-denial and self-sacrifice ruling the heart. How evident is it, then, that a mighty, supernatural work of divine grace must be wrought in the human heart if any man will even desire to meet such terms!

The sixth passage tells us that the Christian is to continue as he began. We are to "come to Christ" not once and for all, but frequently, daily. He is the only One who can minister to our needs, and to Him we must constantly turn for the supply of them. In our felt emptiness, we must draw from His fullness (John 1:16). In our weakness we must turn to Him for strength. In our ignorance we must seek afresh His cleansing. All that we need for time and eternity is stored up in Him: refreshment when we are weary (Isaiah 40:31), healing of body when we are sick (Exodus 15:26), comfort when we are sad (1 Peter 5:7), and deliverance when we are tempted (Hebrews 2:18). If we have wandered away from Him, left our first love, then the remedy is to "repent and do the first works" (Revelation 2:5), that is, cast ourselves upon Him anew, come just as we did the first time we came to Him—as unworthy, self-confessed sinners, seeking His mercy and forgiveness.

The seventh passage assures us of the eternal security of those who do come. Christ saves "unto the uttermost" or "for evermore" those who come unto God by Him. He is not of one mind today and of another tomorrow. No, He is "the same yesterday, today, and forever" (Hebrews 13:8). "Having loved his own which were in the world, He loved them unto the end" (John 13:1), and blessedly does He give proof of this, for "He ever liveth to make intercession for them." Inasmuch as His prayers are effectual, for He declares that the Father hears Him always (John 11:42), none whose name is indelibly stamped on the heart of our great High Priest can ever perish. Hallelujah!

Having sought to thus introduce some of the leading aspects of the subject that is to engage our attention, we now propose to enter into some detail as the Spirit of Truth is pleased to grant us His much-needed assistance. Let us consider some of the obstacles in coming to Christ.

9

Obstacles in Coming to Christ

Under this heading it will be my endeavor to show why it is that the natural man is unable to come to Christ. As a starting point let me again quote John 6:44: "No man can come to Me except the Father which hath sent Me draw him." The reason why this is such a hard saying, even unto thousands who profess to be Christians, is because they utterly fail to realize the terrible havoc that the Fall has wrought, and, it is greatly to be feared, because they are themselves strangers to "the plague" of their own hearts (1 Kings 8:38). Surely if the Spirit had ever awakened them from the sleep of spiritual death, and given them to see something of the dreadful state they were in by nature, and if they had been brought to feel that the carnal mind in them was "enmity against God" (Romans 8:7), then they would no longer cavil against this solemn word of Christ's. But the spiritually dead can neither see nor feel spiritually.

So wherein does the total inability of the natural man lie?

1. It is not in the lack of the necessary faculties. This needs to be plainly insisted upon, or otherwise fallen man would cease to be a responsible creature. Fearful as were the effects of the Fall, yet they deprived man of none of the faculties with which God originally endowed him. It is true that the coming in of sin took away from man all power to use those faculties aright, that is, to employ them for the glory of his Maker. Nevertheless, fallen man possesses identically the same threefold nature—of

75

spirit and soul and body—as he did before the Fall. No part of man's being was annihilated, though each part was defiled and corrupted by sin. True, man died spiritually, but death is not extinction of being. Spiritual death is alienation from God (Ephesians 4:18); the spiritually dead one is very much alive and active in the service of Satan.

No, the inability of fallen man to come to Christ lies in no physical or mental defect. He has the same feet to take him to a place where the gospel is preached as he has to walk with to a picture show. He has the same eyes by which to read the Holy Scriptures as he has to read the world's newspapers. He has the same lips and voice for calling upon God as he now uses in idle talk or foolish songs. So too he has the same mental faculties for pondering the things of God and the concerns of eternity as he now uses so diligently in connection with his business. It is because of this that man is without excuse. It is the misuse of the faculties with which the Creator has endowed him that increases man's guilt. Let every servant of God see to it that these things are constantly pressed upon their unsaved hearers.

2. We have to search deeper in order to find the seat of man's spiritual impotence. His inability lies in his corrupt nature. Through Adam's fall, and through our own sin, our nature has become so debased and depraved that it is impossible for any to "come to Christ," to "love and serve Him," to esteem Him more highly than all the world put together and submit to His rule, until the Spirit of God renews him and implants a new nature in him. A bitter fountain cannot send forth sweet waters, nor can an evil tree produce good fruit. Let me try and make this still clearer by an illustration. It is the nature of a vulture to feed upon carrion. True, it has the same bodily members to feed upon the wholesome grain as the hens do, but it lacks the disposition and relish for it. It is the nature of a sow to wallow in the

mire. True, it has the same legs as a sheep to conduct it to the meadow, but it lacks the desire for the green pastures. So it is with the unregenerate man. He has the same physical and mental faculties as the regenerate have for the things and service of God, but he has no love for them.

"Adam. . .begat a son in his own likeness, after his image" (Genesis 5:3). What an awful contrast is found here from that which we read two verses before: "God created man, in the likeness of God made he him." In the interval, Adam had fallen, and a fallen parent could beget only a fallen child, transmitting unto him his own depravity. "Who can bring a clean thing out of an unclean?" (Job 14:4). Therefore do we find the sweet singer of Israel declaring, "Behold I was shapen in iniquity, and in sin did my mother conceive me" (Psalm 51:5). Though, later, grace made him the man after God's own heart, yet by nature David (as we) was a mass of iniquity and sin. How early this corruption of nature appears in children. "Even a child is known by his doings" (Proverbs 20:11). The evil bias of its heart is soon manifested. Pride, self-will, vanity, lying, and averseness to good are the bitter fruits that quickly appear on the tender but vitiated twig.

3. The inability of the natural man to "come to Christ" lies in the complete darkness of his understanding. This leading faculty of the soul has been spoiled of its primitive glory, and covered over with confusion. Both mind and conscience are defiled. "There is none that understandeth" (Romans 3:11). Solemnly did the apostle remind the saints: "Ye were sometimes darkness" (Ephesians 5:8), not merely "in darkness," but "darkness" itself.

Thomas Boston wrote, "Sin has closed the windows of the soul, darkness is over all the region; it is the land of darkness and the shadow of death, where the light is as darkness. The prince of darkness reigns there, and nothing but the works of darkness are framed there. We are born spiritually blind, and cannot be restored without a miracle of grace. This is thy case, whoever thou art, that art not born again." "They are wise to do evil, but to do good they have no knowledge" (Jeremiah 4:22).

"The carnal mind is enmity against God, for it is not subject to the law of God, neither indeed can be" (Romans 8:7). There is in the unregenerate an opposition to spiritual things and an aversion against them. God has made a revelation of His will unto sinners touching the way of salvation, yet they will not walk therein. They hear that Christ alone is able to save, yet they refuse to part with those things that hinder their coming to Him. They hear that it is sin that slays the soul, and yet they cherish it in their bosoms. They do not heed the threatenings of God. Men believe that fire will burn them, and are at great pains to avoid it; yet they show by their actions that they regard the everlasting burnings as a mere scarecrow. The divine commandments are "holy, just, and good," but men hate them, and observe them only so far as their respectability among men is promoted.

4. The inability of the natural man to "come to Christ" lies in the complete corruption of his affections. Charles Spurgeon, in a sermon on John 6:44, said, "Man as he is, before he receives the grace of God, loves anything and everything above spiritual things. If you want proof of this, look around you. There needs no monument to the depravity of the human affections. Cast your eyes everywhere—there is not a street, nor a house, nay, nor a heart, that does not bear upon it sad evidence of this dreadful truth. Why is it that men are not found on the Sabbath day universally flocking to the house of God? Why are we not more constantly found reading our Bibles? How is it that prayer is a duty that is almost universally neglected? Why is Christ Jesus so

little beloved? Why are even His professed followers so cold in their affections to Him? Whence arise these things? Assuredly, dear brethren, we can trace them to no other source than this, the corruption and vitiation of the affections. We love that which we ought to hate, and we hate that which we ought to love. It is but human nature, fallen human nature, that man should love this present life better than the life to come. It is but the effect of the Fall that man should love sin better than right-eousness, and the ways of this world better than the ways of God."

The affections of the unrenewed man are wholly depraved and distempered. "The heart is deceitful above all things, and desperately wicked" (Jeremiah 17:9). Solemnly did the Lord Je-sus affirm that the affections of fallen man are a mother of abominations: "For from within (not from the devil!), out of the heart of men, proceed evil thoughts, adulteries, fornications, murders, thefts, covetousness, wickedness, deceit, lasciviousness, an evil eye, blasphemy, pride, foolishness" (Mark 7:21-22).

Thomas Boston wrote in his *Human Nature in Its Fourfold State*: "The natural man's affections are wretchedly misplaced; he is a spiritual monster. His heart is where his feet should be, fixed on the earth; his heels are lifted up against heaven, which his heart should be set on (Acts 9:5). His face is towards hell, his back towards heaven; and therefore God calls him to turn. He joys in what he ought to mourn for, and mourns for what he should rejoice in. He glories in his shame, and is ashamed of his glory; he abhors what he should desire, and desires what he should abhor (Proverbs 2:13-15)."

5. The inability of the natural man to "come to Christ" lies in the total depravity of his will. Again, to quote Spurgeon: " 'Oh!' says the Arminian, 'men may be saved if they will.' We reply, 'My dear sir, we all believe that; but it is just the "if they

will" that is the difficulty.' We assert that no man will come to Christ unless he be drawn; nay, we do not assert it, but Christ Himself declares it—'Ye will not come to me that ye might have life' (John 5:40); and as long as that "ye will not come" stands on record in Holy Scripture, we shall not be brought to believe in any doctrine of the freedom of the human will. It is strange how people, when talking about free-will, talk of things which they do not at all understand. 'Now,' says one, 'I believe men can be saved if they will.' My dear sir, that is not the question at all. The question is, are men ever found naturally willing to submit to the humbling terms of the gospel of Christ? We declare upon scriptural authority that the human will is so desperately set on mischief, so depraved, and so inclined to everything that is evil, and so disinclined to everything that is good, that without the powerful, supernatural, irresistible influence of the Holy Spirit, no human being will ever be constrained towards Christ."

Thomas Boston: "Now here is a threefold cord against heaven and holiness, not easily to be broken—a blind mind, a perverse will, and disorderly, distempered affections. The mind, swelled with self-conceit, says the man should not stoop; and the corrupt affections rising against the Lord, in defense of the corrupt will, says, he shall not. Thus the poor creature stands out against God and goodness, till a day of power comes in which he is made a new creature."

Perhaps some readers are inclined to say that such teaching as this is calculated to discourage sinners and drive them to despair. My answer is, first, it is according to God's Word! Second, oh, that it may please Him to use this article to drive some to despair of all help from themselves. Third, it makes manifest the absolute necessity of the Holy Spirit's working with such depraved and spiritually helpless creatures, if they are ever to savingly come to Christ. And until this is clearly perceived, His aid will never be really sought in earnest!

There are some souls greatly distressed and puzzled to know exactly what is signified by "coming to Christ." They have read and heard the words often, and perhaps many a preacher has bidden them to come to Him, yet without giving a scriptural explanation of what that term connotes. Such as have been awakened by the Spirit, shown their woeful condition, convicted of their high-handed and lifelong rebellion against God, and brought to realize their dire need of Christ, and who are truly anxious to come savingly to Him, have found it a task altogether beyond their powers. Their cry is, "Oh, that I knew where I might find Him, that I might come even to His seat!" (Job 23:3). True, there are not many who pass through such an experience, for God's flock is but a little one (Luke 12:32). True, the vast majority of professing Christians claim that they found "coming to Christ" a very simple matter. But in the clear light of John 6:44 I must assure you, dear reader, that if you found "coming to Christ" to be easy, then it is proof you have never come to Him at all in a spiritual and saving way.

What, then, is meant by "coming to Christ"? First, and negatively, let it be pointed out that it is not an act that we perform by any of our bodily members. This is so obvious that there should be no need for me to make the statement. But in these awful days of spiritual ignorance, and the carnal perversion of the holy things of God, explanation of the most elementary truths and terms is really required. When so many precious souls have been deluded into thinking that a going forward to a "mourner's bench" or "penitent form," or the taking of some preacher's hand, is the same thing as coming to Christ, I dare not pass over the defining of this apparently simple term, nor ignore the need for pointing out what it does not signify.

Second, the word "come," when used in this connection, is a metaphorical one; that is to say, it is a word that expresses an act of the body that is transferred to the soul. To "come to Christ" signifies the movement of a Spirit-enlightened mind toward the Lord Jesus—as Prophet, to be instructed by Him; as Priest, whose atonement and intercession are to be relied upon; as King, to be ruled by Him. Coming to Christ implies a turning of our back upon the world, and a turning unto Him as our only hope and portion. It is a going out of self so as to rest no longer on anything in self. It is the abandoning of every idol and of all other dependencies, the heart going out to Him in loving submission and trustful confidence. It is the will surrendering to Him as Lord, ready to accept His yoke, take up the cross, and follow Him without reserve.

To "come to Christ" is the turning of the whole soul unto a whole Christ in the exercise of divine grace upon Him; it is the mind, heart, and will being supernaturally drawn to Him so as to trust, love, and serve Him. As Matthew Henry wrote: "It is the duty and interest of weary and heavy-laden sinners to 'come to Jesus Christ'—renouncing all those things that stand in opposition to Him, or in competition with Him; we must accept Him as our Physician and Advocate, and give up ourselves to His conduct and government, freely willing to be saved by Him, in His own way and on His own terms."

Before proceeding further, I would earnestly beg each reader to prayerfully and carefully test and measure himself of herself by what has been said in this and the preceding paragraph. Take nothing for granted; as you value your soul, seek divine help to make sure that you have truly "come to Christ."

Now a Romanist's "Christ" is a Christ of wood; and a false preacher's "Christ" is a Christ of words; but Christ Jesus, our Lord, is "the mighty God, the everlasting Father, the Prince of peace" (Isaiah 9:6). The Christ of God fills heaven and earth. He is the One by whom all things exist and consist. He is seated at the right hand of the Majesty on high, having all power, dominion, and might. He is made higher than the heavens, and unto Him all principalities and powers are subject. At His presence both the earth and the heavens shall yet flee away. Such a Christ is neither to be offered nor proffered, sold nor given by sinful men. He is the unspeakable gift of the Father to as many as He has ordained to eternal life, and none others. This Christ, this gift of the Father, is supernaturally revealed and applied to the heirs of salvation by the Holy Spirit, when, where, and as He pleases, and not when, where, and how men please.

In the preceding article I dwelt at length upon those words of Christ in John 6:44, "No man can come unto Me," seeking to show the nature of the fallen creature's spiritual impotence, or why it is that the unregenerate are unable to come to Christ in a spiritual and saving way. Let us now ponder the remainder of our Lord's sentence: "except the Father which sent Me draw him." Of what does that "drawing" consist? I answer, first, just as our "coming to Christ" does not refer to any bodily action, so this divine "drawing" does not respect the employment of any external force. Second, it signifies a powerful impulse put forth by the Holy Spirit within the elect, whereby their native impotence for performing spiritual actions is overcome, and an ability for the same is imparted. It is this secret and effectual operation of the Spirit upon the human soul that enables and causes it to come to Christ. And this brings us to our next division.

10

Coming to Christ With Our Understanding

1. A knowledge of Christ is essential. There can be no movement towards an unknown object. No man can obey a command until he is acquainted with its terms. A prop must be seen before it will be rested upon. We must have some acquaintance with a person before he will either be trusted or loved. This principle is so obvious it needs arguing no further. Apply it unto the case in hand, the subject before us: the knowledge of Christ must of necessity precede our believing on Him or our coming to Him. "How shall they believe in Him of whom they have not heard?" (Romans 10:14). "He that cometh to God must believe that He is, and that He is a rewarder of them that diligently seek Him" (Hebrews 11:6). None can come to Christ while they are ignorant about Him. As it was in the old creation, so it is in the new: God first says, "Let there be light."

2. This knowledge of Christ comes to the mind from the Holy Scriptures. Nothing can be known of Him save that which God has been pleased to reveal concerning Him in the Word of Truth. It is there alone that the true doctrine of Christ (2 John 9) is to be found. Therefore did our Lord give commandment, "Search the Scriptures. . .they are they which testify of me" (John 5:39). When He berated the two disciples for their slowness of heart to believe, we are told that, "beginning at Moses

and all the prophets, He expounded unto them in all the scriptures the things concerning Himself" (Luke 24:27). The divine
Oracles are designed "the word of Christ" (Colossians 3:16) because He is the substance of them. Where the Scriptures have
not gone, Christ is unknown; clear proof is this that an acquaintance with Him cannot be gained apart from their inspired testimony.

3. A theoretical knowledge of Christ is not sufficient. Upon
this point I must dilate at greater length, for much ignorance
concerning it prevails today. A head-knowledge about Christ is
very frequently mistaken for a heart-acquaintance with Him. But
orthodoxy is not salvation. A carnal judgment about Christ, a
mere intellectual knowledge of Him, will never bring a dead
sinner to His feet; there must be a living experience, God's
Word and work meeting together in the soul, renewing and understanding. As 1 Corinthians 13:2 so plainly and solemnly
warns us, I may have the gift of prophecy, understand all myster-
ies, and all knowledge, yet if I have not love, then I am nothing.
Just as a blind man may, through labor and diligence, acquire an
accurate theoretical or notional conception of many subjects
and objects that he never saw, so the natural man may, by religious education and personal effort, obtain a sound doctrinal
knowledge of the person and work of Christ without having any
spiritual or vital acquaintance with Him.

Not every kind of knowledge, even God's Truth and His
Christ, is effectual and saving. There is a form of knowledge, as
well as of godliness, that is destitute of power—"which hast the
form of knowledge and of the truth in the law" (Romans 2:20).
The reference is to the Jews, who were instructed in the Scriptures, and considered themselves well qualified to teach others;
yet the truth had not been written on their hearts by the Holy
Spirit. A "form of knowledge" signifies there was a model of it

in their brains, so that they were able to discourse freely and fluently upon the things of God, yet were they without the life of God in their souls. Oh, how many have a knowledge of salvation, yet not a knowledge unto salvation, as the apostle distinguishes it in 2 Timothy 3:15. Such a knowledge as the latter must be imparted to the soul by the miracle-working operation of the Holy Spirit.

"They proceed from evil to evil, and they know not me, saith the Lord" (Jeremiah 9:3). Of whom was this spoken, of the heathen who were without any written revelation from Him? No, of Israel, who had His law in their hands, His temple in their midst, and His prophets speaking to them. They had been favored with many and wondrous manifestations of His majesty, holiness, power, and mercy; yet though they had much intellectual knowledge of Him, they were strangers to Him spiritually. So it was when the Son of God became incarnate. How much natural light they had concerning Him: they witnessed His perfect life, saw His wondrous miracles, heard His matchless teaching, and were frequently in His immediate presence; yet, though the Light shone in the darkness, "the darkness comprehended it not" (John 1:5). So it is today. Reader, you may be a diligent student of the New Testament, be thoroughly acquainted with the Old Testament types and prophecies, believe all that the Scriptures say concerning Christ, and earnestly teach them to others, and yet be yourself a stranger to Him spiritually.

"Except a man be born again, he cannot see the kingdom of God" (John 3:3), which means that the unregenerate are utterly incapable of discerning the things of God spiritually. True, they may "see" them in a natural way; they may investigate and even admire them theoretically, but to receive them in an experimental and vital way they cannot do.

As this distinction is of such great importance, and yet so little known today, let me endeavor to illustrate it. Suppose there was a man who had never heard any music; others tell him of its beauty and charm, and he decides to make a careful study of it. That man might thoroughly familiarize himself with the art of music, learn all the rules of that art, so that he understood the proportions and harmony of it; but what a different thing is that from listening to a grand oratorio—the ear now taking in what before the mind knew only the theory of! Still greater is the difference between a natural and a spiritual knowledge of divine things.

The apostle declared, "We speak the wisdom of God in a mystery" (1 Corinthians 2:7). He did not only affirm that it is a mystery in itself, but that it is still spoken "in a mystery." And why is this? Because the unregenerate, even where it is spoken in their hearing, yea, when it is clearly apprehended by them in a notional way, yet they neither know nor apprehend the mystery that is still in it. Proverbs 9:10 declares, "The knowledge of the holy is understanding." There is no true understanding of divine things except the "knowledge of the Holy." Every real Christian has a knowledge of divine things, a personal, experimental, vital knowledge of them, which no carnal man possesses, or can obtain, no matter how diligently he studies them. If I have seen the picture of a man, I have an image in my mind of that man according to his picture; but if I see the man himself, how different is the image of him that is then formed in my mind! Far greater still is the difference between Christ made known in the Scriptures and Christ revealed "in me" (Galatians 1:16).

4. There must be a spiritual and supernatural knowledge of Christ imparted by the Holy Spirit. This is in view in 1 John 5:20: "We know that the Son of God is come, and hath given us

an understanding, that we may know Him that is true." The
faculty must be suited to the object or subject known. The natural understanding is capable of taking in Christ and knowing
Him in a natural way, but we must be renewed in the spirit of
our mind (Ephesians 4:23) before we can know Christ in a spiritual way. There must be a supernatural work of grace wrought
upon the mind by the Holy Spirit before there can be any inward and spiritual apprehension of the supernatural and spiritual person of Christ. That is the true and saving knowledge of
Christ which fires the affections, sanctifies the will, and raises
up the mind to a spiritual fixation on the Rock of ages. It is this
knowledge of Him that is "life eternal" (John 17:3). It is this
knowledge that produces faith in Christ, love for Him, and
submission to Him. It is this knowledge that causes the soul to
truthfully and joyously exclaim, "Whom have I in heaven but
Thee? And there is none upon earth that I desire beside Thee"
(Psalm 73:25).

"No man can come unto Me, except the Father which hath
sent Me draw him" (John 6:44). It is by the secret and effectual
operation of the Spirit that the Father brings each of His elect to
a saving knowledge of Christ. These operations of the Spirit begin by His enlightening the understanding, renewing the mind.
Observe carefully the order in Ezekiel 37:14: "And shall put My
Spirit in you, and ye shall live. . .then shall ye know that I the
Lord have spoken it." No sinner ever comes to Christ until the
Holy Spirit first comes to him! And no sinner will savingly believe on Christ until the Spirit has communicated faith to him
(Ephesians 2:5; Colossians 2:12); and even then faith is an eye
to discern Christ before it is a foot to approach Him. There can
be no act without an object, and there can be no exercising of
faith upon Christ till Christ is seen in His excellence, sufficiency, and suitability to poor sinners. "They that know Thy

name will (not "ought to") put their trust in Thee" (Psalm 9:10). But again, we say, that knowledge must be a spiritual and miraculous one imparted by the Spirit.

The Spirit Himself, and not merely a preacher, must take the things of Christ and show them unto the heart. It is only in God's "light" that we truly "see light" (Psalm 36:9). The opening of his eyes precedes the conversion of the sinner from Satan unto God (Acts 26:18). The light of the sun is seen breaking out at the dawn of day before its heat is felt. It is those who "see" the Son with a supernaturally enlightened understanding that "believe" on Him with a spiritual and saving faith (John 6:40). We behold as in a mirror the glory of the Lord before we are changed into His very image (2 Corinthians 3:18). Note the order in Romans 3:11: "There is none that understandeth" goes before "there is none that seeketh after God." The Spirit must shed His light upon the understanding, which light conveys the actual image of spiritual things in a spiritual way to the mind, forming them on the soul; much as a sensitive photographic plate receives from the light the images to which it is exposed. This is the "demonstration of the Spirit and of power" (1 Corinthians 2:4).

5. How is this spiritual and vital knowledge to be known from a mere theoretical and notional one? By its effects. Unto the Thessalonians Paul wrote: "For our gospel came not unto you in word only, but also in power, and in the Holy Ghost, and in much assurance" (1 Thessalonians 1:5), which is partly explained in the next verse, "having received the word in much affliction, with joy of the Holy Ghost." The Spirit had given that Word an efficacy that no logic, rhetoric, or persuasive power of men could. It had smitten the conscience, torn open the wounds that sin had made, and exposed its festering sores. It had pierced them even to the dividing asunder of soul and

spirit. It had slain their good opinion of themselves. It had
made them feel the wrath of God burning against them. It had
caused them to seriously question if such wretches could possibly find mercy at the hands of a holy God. It had communicated
faith to look upon the great physician of souls. It had given a joy
such as this poor world knows nothing of.

The light that the Spirit imparts to the understanding is full
of efficacy, whereas that which men acquire through their study
is not so. Ordinary and strong mineral water are alike in color,
but differ much in their taste and virtue. A carnal man may acquire a theoretical knowledge of all that a spiritual man knows
vitally, yet is he "barren and unfruitful in the knowledge of our
Lord Jesus Christ" (2 Peter 1:8). The light that he has is ineffec-
tual, for it neither purifies his heart, renews his will, nor transforms his life. The head-knowledge of divine truth, which is all
that multitudes of present-day professing Christians possess, has
no more influence upon their walk unto practical godliness than
if it was stored up in some other man's brains. The light that the
Spirit gives humbles and abases its recipient; the knowledge that
is acquired by education and personal efforts puffs up and fills
with conceit.

A spiritual and saving knowledge of Christ always constrains
the soul unto loving obedience. No sooner did the light of
Christ shine into Paul's heart than he at once asked, "Lord,
what wilt Thou have me to do?" (Acts 9:6). Of the Colossians
the apostle declared, "The gospel which is come unto you. . .
bringeth forth fruit. . .since the day ye heard. . .and knew the
grace of God in truth" or "in reality" (Colossians 1:6). But a
mere intellectual knowledge of the truth is held in unrighteousness (Romans 1:18). Its possessors are zealous to argue and cavil
about it, and look down with contempt upon all who are not so
wise as they; yet the lives of these frequently put them to shame.

A saving knowledge of Christ so endears Him to the soul that all else is esteemed as dung in comparison with His excellence; the light of His glory has cast a complete eclipse over all that is in the world. But a mere doctrinal knowledge of Christ produces no such effects. While its possessors may loudly sing His praises, yet their hearts are still coveting and eagerly pursuing the things of time and sense.

The natural man may know the truth of the things of God, but not the things themselves. He may thoroughly understand the Scriptures in the letter of them, but not in their spirit. He may discourse of them in a sound and orthodox manner, but in no other way than one can talk of honey and vinegar who never tasted the sweetness of the one, nor the sourness of the other. There are hundreds of preachers who have accurate notions of spiritual things, but who neither see nor taste the things themselves that are wrapped in the words of truth—"understanding neither what they say, nor whereof they affirm" (1 Timothy 1:7). Just as an astronomer who makes a life-study of the stars knows their names, positions, and varying magnitudes, yet receives no more personal and special influence from them than do other men, so it is with those who study the Scriptures, but are not supernaturally and savingly enlightened by the Spirit. O my reader, has the Day-star arisen in your heart (2 Peter 1:19)?

I trust that sufficient has been said in the previous articles to make clear unto every Christian reader that the saving "coming to Christ" of a poor sinner is neither a physical nor mental act, but is wholly spiritual and supernatural; that that act springs not from human reason or human willpower, but from the secret and efficacious operations of God the Spirit. I say unto "the Christian reader," for we must not expect the unregenerate to perceive that of which they have no personal experience. The distinction pointed out in the second half of the last article (the

whole of which may well be carefully re-read) between a sound
intellectual knowledge of Christ and a vital and transforming
knowledge of Him, between knowing Christ as He is set forth in
the Scriptures, and as He is divinely revealed in us (Galatians
1:16), is not one that will appeal to the carnal mind. Rather is it
one that will be contemptuously rejected. But instead of being
surprised at this, we should expect it.

If my last article were to be sent to the average "Fundamentalist" preacher or "Bible teacher," and a request made for his
honest opinion of it, in all probability he would say that the
writer had lapsed into either "mysticism" or "fanaticism." Just as
the religious leaders of Christ's day rejected His spiritual teachings, so the "champions of orthodoxy," those who boast so
loudly that they are faithfully and earnestly contending for the
faith, will not receive the humbling and searching messages of
Christ's servants today. The substance of this article would be
ridiculed by them. But their very ridicule only serves to demon-
strate the solemn truth of 1 Corinthians 2:14: "But the natural
man receiveth not the things of the Spirit of God, for they are
foolishness unto him." These words have puzzled some who
have thoughtfully pondered them, for they do not seem to
square with the patent facts of observation.

I have personally met the most conscienceless men—
untruthful, dishonest, not scrupling to use tactics that many a
non-professor would scorn—who, nevertheless, ardently proclaimed the divine inspiration of the Scriptures, the deity of
Christ, and salvation by grace alone. I have had personal dealings with men whose hearts were filled with covetousness, and
whose ways were worldly almost to the last degree, yet who ti-
raded against "modernism" and "evolutionism," and "faithfully
preached" the virgin-birth and the blood of Christ as the sinner's only hope. That these men are "natural" or "carnal," that

is, unregenerate, is plain and unmistakable if we measure them by the infallible rule of Holy Writ. It would not only be a contradiction in terms, but blasphemy to say such had been made by God "new creatures in Christ." Nevertheless, so far from the foundational truths of Scripture being "foolishness" unto these unregenerate characters, they warmly endorse and ardently propagate them.

But what has been said above does not clash, to the slightest degree, with 1 Corinthians 2:14, when that verse is rightly read and understood. Let it be carefully noted that it does not say the "things of God are foolishness" unto the natural man. Had it done so, the writer would have been at a complete loss to explain it. No, it declares that the "things of the Spirit of God" are foolishness; and what has been said above only serves to illustrate the minute accuracy of this verse. The "things of God" these men profess to believe, the "things of Christ" they appear to valiantly champion; but the "things of the Spirit of God" they are personal strangers unto. And therefore, when His secret and mysterious work upon the souls of God's elect is pressed upon them, they appear to be so much "foolishness" unto them—either "mysticism" or "fanaticism." But to the renewed it is far otherwise.

The Spirit's supernatural operations in the implanting of faith in God's elect (Colossians 2:12) produce a "new creation." Salvation by faith is wrought through the Spirit's working effectually with the gospel. Then it is that He forms Christ in the soul (Galatians 4:19), and lets the Object of faith through the eye of faith, a real "image" of Christ being directly stamped upon the newly-quickening soul, which quickening has given ability to discern Christ. Thus, Christ is "formed" in the heart, after the manner that an outward object is formed in the eye. When I say that I have a certain man or object in my eye, I do not mean that this man or object is in my eye locally—that is impossible; but they are in my eye objectively—I see them. So, when it is said that Christ is "formed in us," that Christ is in us "the hope of glory" (Colossians 1:27), it is not to be understood that He who is now corporeally at the right hand of God is locally and substantially formed in us. No, but that Christ at the right hand of God, the substance and Object of faith, is by the Spirit let in from above, so that the soul sees Him by the eye of faith exactly as He is represented in the Word. So Christ is "formed" in us; and thus He dwells in our hearts by faith (Ephesians 3:17).

What I have endeavored to set forth above is beautifully adumbrated in the lower and visible world. It is indeed striking to discover how much of God's spiritual works are shadowed out in the material realm. If our minds were but more spiritual, and our eyes engaged in a keener lookout, we would find signs and symbols on every side of the invisible realities of God. On a sunshiny day, when a man looks into clear water, he sees there a face (his own), formed by representation, which directly answers to the face outside and above the water; there are not two faces, but one, original and yet represented. But only one face is seen, casting its own single image upon the water. So it is in the soul's history of God's elect. "But we all, with open face beholding as in a glass the glory of the Lord, are changed into the same image from glory to glory, even as by the Spirit of the Lord" (2 Corinthians 3:18). Oh, that His image in us may be more evident to others!

11

Coming to Christ With Our Affections

"All that the Father giveth Me shall come to Me" (John 6:37), declared the Lord Jesus. He who, before the foundation of the world, gave the persons of His people unto Christ, now gives them, in regeneration, a heart for Christ. The "heart" includes the affections as well as the understanding. In the previous chapter I pointed out how that no man will (or can) "come to Christ" while ignorant of Him; it is equally true that no man will (or can) "come to Christ" while his affections are alienated from Him. Not only is the understanding of the natural man shrouded in total darkness, but his heart is thoroughly opposed to God. "The carnal mind is enmity (not merely "at enmity," but "enmity" itself) against God" (Romans 8:7)—and "enmity" is something more than a train of hostile thoughts, it is the hatred of the affections themselves. Therefore, when the Holy Spirit makes a man a "new creature in Christ," He not only renews his understanding, but He radically changes the heart.

When faith gives us a sight of spiritual things, the heart is warmed with love for them. Note the order in Hebrews 11:13 where, in connection with the patriarchs' faith in God's promises, we are told, "were persuaded of them, and embraced them," which is a term denoting great affection. When the understanding is renewed by the Spirit, then the heart is drawn

unto Christ with a tender desire for Him. When the Holy Spirit
is pleased to make known in the soul the wondrous love of
Christ for me, then love for Him is begotten and goes out toward Him in return. Observe the order in 1 John 4:16: "And we
have known and believed the love that God hath to us. God is
love; and he that dwelleth in love dwelleth in God, and God in
him." The apostle places knowledge (not intellectual, but spiritual) before faith, and both before a union and communion
with divine love. The light and knowledge of Christ and heaven
that we have by tradition, education, hearing, or reading never
fires the affections. But when the love of God is "shed abroad in
our hearts by the Holy Ghost" (Romans 5:5), oh, what a difference is produced!

Far too little emphasis has been placed upon this aspect of
our subject. In proof of this assertion, weigh carefully the following question: Why is it that "he that believeth not shall be
damned" (Mark 16:16) is quoted a hundred times more frequently by preachers and tract writers than "if any man love not
the Lord Jesus Christ, let him be anathema" (1 Corinthians
16:22)? If we are to properly preserve the balance of truth, we
must note carefully the manner in which the Holy Spirit has
rung the changes on "believe" and "love" in the New Testament.
Consider the following verses: "All things work together for
good to them that (not "trust," but) love God" (Romans 8:28);
"the things which God hath prepared for them that (not only
"believe," but) love Him" (1 Corinthians 2:9); "if any love God,
the same is known (or "approved") of Him" (1 Corinthians 8:3);
"a crown of righteousness, which the Lord, the righteous judge,
shall give me in that day: and not to me only, but unto all them
also that (not "believe in," but) love His appearing" (2 Timothy
4:8); "the crown of life which the Lord hath promised to them

that love Him" (James 1:12); "He that loveth not knoweth not God; for God is love" (1 John 4:8).

"No man can come to Me, except the Father which hath sent Me draw him" (John 6:44). In the last chapter we saw that this "drawing" consists, in part, of the Spirit's supernatural enlightenment of the understanding. It also consists in the Spirit's inclining the affections unto Christ. He acts upon sinners agreeably to their nature—not by external force, such as is used on an unwilling animal, but by spiritual influence or power moving their inward faculties. "I drew them with cords of a man, with bands of love" (Hosea 11:4)—by rational conviction of their judgment, by showing them that there is infinitely more goodness and blessedness in Christ than in the creature or the sinful gratification of carnal desire; by winning their hearts to Christ, by communicating to them a powerful sense of His superlative excellence and complete suitability unto all their needs. To them who believe, "He is precious" (1 Peter 2:7), so precious that they are willing to part with the world and everything that they may "win Christ" (Philippians 3:8).

As was shown at some length in the opening chapter, the affections of the natural man are alienated from God, wedded to the things of time and sense, so that he will not come to Christ. Though God's servants seek to charm him with the lovely music of the gospel, like the adder he closes his ear. It is as the Lord portrayed it in the parable of the Great Supper: "They all with one consent began to make excuse" (Luke 14:18), one preferring his lands, another his merchandise, another his social recreation. And nothing short of the almighty power and working of the Holy Spirit in the heart can break the spell that sin and Satan has cast over man, and turn his heart from perishing objects to an imperishable one. This He does in God's elect by His secret and invincible operations, sweetly working in and alluring them by revealing Christ to them in the winsomeness of His person and the infinite riches of His grace, by letting down His love into their hearts, and by moving them to lay hold of His kind invitations and precious promises.

Most blessedly is this represented to us in "My beloved put in his hand by the hole of the door, and my bowels were moved for him" (Song of Solomon 5:4). Here the door of the heart (Acts 16:14), or more specifically, the "door of faith" (Acts 14:27), is seen shut against Christ, and the object of His love being so loath and unwilling as to rise and open to Him. But though unwelcome, His love cannot be quenched, and He gently enters (He does not burst the door open!) uninvited. His "hand" opening the "door" is a figure of His efficacious grace removing every obstacle in the heart of His elect (cf. Acts 11:21), and winning it to Himself. The effect of His gracious entry, by His Spirit, is seen in the "and my bowels were moved for him," which is a figure of the stirring of the affections after Him (cf. Isaiah 63:15; Philemon 12). For the thoughts of this paragraph I am indebted to the incomparable commentary of John Gill on the Song of Solomon.

Oh, what a miracle of grace has been wrought when the heart is truly turned from the world unto God, from self unto Christ, from love of sin unto love of holiness! It is this that is the fulfillment of God's covenant promise in Ezekiel 36:26: "A new heart also will I give you, and a new spirit will I put within you; and I will take away the stony heart out of your flesh, and I will give you an heart of flesh." There is no man that loves money so much but that he is willing to part with it for that which he values more highly than the sum he parts with to purchase it. The natural man esteems material things more highly than he does spiritual, but the regenerated person loves Christ more than all other objects beside, and this because he has been made a "new creature." It is a spiritual love that binds the heart to Christ.

It is not simply a knowledge of the truth that saves, but a love of it that is the essential prerequisite. This is clear from 2 Thessalonians 2:10: "Because they received not the love of the truth, that they might be saved." Close attention must be paid unto these words, or a wrong conclusion may be drawn. It is not a love *for* the truth, but a love *of* the truth. There are those who have the former who are destitute of the latter. I have met Russelites (Jehovah's Witnesses), and have boarded with Christadelphians (deniers of the deity of Christ and a literal hell), who put many a real Christian to shame, people who after a long day's work, spent the whole evening in diligently studying the Bible. Nor was it just to satisfy curiosity. Their zeal had lasted for years. Their Bible was as precious to them as a devout Romanist's beads or rosary are to him or her. So too there is a natural "love" for Christ, an ardent devotion for Him, that does not spring from a renewed heart. Just as one reared among devout Romanists grows up with a deep veneration and genuine affection for the Virgin Mary, so one carefully trained by Protestant parents, told from infancy that Jesus loves him, grows up with a real but natural love for Him.

There may be a historical faith in all the doctrines of Scripture, where the power of them is never experienced. There may be a fleshly zeal for portions of God's truth (as there was in the case of the Pharisees), and yet the heart not be renewed. There may be joyous emotions felt by a superficial reception of the Word (as there was in the stony-ground hearers, Matthew 13:20), where the "root of the matter" (Job 19:28) is lacking. Tears may flow freely at the pathetic sight of the suffering Savior (as with the company of women who bewailed Christ as He journeyed to the cross, Luke 23:27-28), and yet the heart be as hard as the nether millstone toward God. There may be a rejoicing in the light of God's truth (as was the case with Herod in Mark 6:20), and yet hell never be escaped from.

Since then there is a love *for* the truth in contradistinction from a love *of* the truth, and a natural love for Christ in contrast from a spiritual love of Him, how am I to be sure which mine is? We may distinguish between these "loves" thus:

First, the one is partial, the other is impartial; the one esteems the doctrines of Scripture, but not the duties it enjoins; the promises of Scripture, but not the precepts; the blessings of Christ, but not His claims; His priestly office, but not His kingly rule. But it is not so with the spiritual lover.

Second, the one is occasional, the other is regular. The former balks when personal interests are crossed; not so the latter.

Third, the one is evanescent and weak, the other lasting and powerful; the former quickly wanes when other delights compete, and does not prevail to control the other affections; the latter rules the heart, and is strong as death.

Fourth, the former betters not its possessor; the latter transforms the life.

That a saving "coming to Christ" is the affections being turned to and fixed upon Him may be further demonstrated from the nature of backsliding, which begins with the heart's departure from Christ. Observe how this is traced to its real source in Revelation 2:4: "Thou hast left (not "lost") thy first love." The reality and genuineness of our returning to Christ is evidenced by the effects that the workings of the understanding produce upon the affections. A striking example of this is found in Matthew 26:75: "And Peter remembered the word of Jesus, which said unto him, 'Before the cock crow, thou shalt deny me thrice.' And he went out, and wept bitterly." That "remembrance" was not merely an historical, but a gracious one—his heart was melted by it. So it ever is when the Holy Spirit works in and "renews" us. I may recall a past sin without being duly humbled thereby. I may "remember" Christ's death in a mechanical and speculative way without the affections being truly moved. It is only as the faculty of our understanding is quickened by the Holy Spirit that the heart is powerfully impressed.

12

Coming to Christ With Our Will

The man within the body is possessed of three principal faculties—the understanding, the affections, and the will. As was shown earlier, all of these were radically affected by the Fall. They were defiled and corrupted, and in consequence, they are used in the service of self and sin, rather than of God and of Christ. But in regeneration, these faculties are quickened and cleansed by the Spirit—not completely, but initially, and continuously so in the life-long process of sanctification, and perfectly so at glorification. Now each of these three faculties is subordinated to the others by the order of nature, that is, as man has been constituted by his Maker. One faculty is influenced by the other. In Genesis 3:6 we read: "The woman saw (perceived) that the tree was good for food"—that was a conclusion drawn by the understanding—"and that it was pleasant to the eyes"—there was the response of her affections—"and a tree to be desired"—there was the moving of the will; and "she took"—there was the completed action.

Now the motions of divine grace work through the apprehensions of faith in the understanding, these warming and firing the affections, and they in turn influencing and moving the will. Every faculty of the soul is put forth in a saving "coming to Christ." "If thou believest with all thine heart, thou mayest" be baptized (Acts 8:37). "Coming to Christ" is more immediately an act of the will, as John 5:40 shows; yet the will is not active toward Him until the understanding has been enlightened and the affections quickened. The Spirit first causes the sinner to perceive his deep need of Christ, and this by showing him his fearful rebellion against God, and that none but Christ can atone for the same. Second, the Spirit creates in the heart a desire after Christ, and this by making him sick of sin and in love with holiness. Third, as the awakened and enlightened soul has been given to see the glory and excellence of Christ, and His perfect suitability to the lost and perishing sinner, then the Spirit draws out the will to set the highest value on that excellence, to esteem it far above all else, and to close with Him.

As there is a divine order among the three Persons of the Godhead in providing salvation, so there is in the applying or bestowing of it. It was God the Father's good pleasure to appoint His people from eternity unto salvation, which was the most full and sufficient impulsive cause of their salvation, and every whit able to produce its effect. It was the incarnate Son of God whose obedience and sufferings were the most complete and sufficient meritorious cause of their salvation, to which nothing can be added to make it more apt and able to secure the travail of His soul. Yet neither the one nor the other can actually save any sinner except as the Spirit applies Christ to it, His work being the efficient and immediate cause of their salvation. In like manner, the sinner is not saved when his understanding is enlightened and his affections fired; there must also be the act of the will, surrendering to God and laying hold of Christ.

The order of the Spirit's operations corresponds to the three great offices of Christ the Mediator, namely His prophetic, priestly, and kingly offices. As Prophet, He is first apprehended

by the understanding, the Truth of God being received from
His lips. As Priest, He is trusted and loved by the heart or affections, His glorious person being first endeared unto the soul by
the gracious work that He performed for it. As Potentate, our
will must be subdued unto Him, so that we submit to His government, yield to His scepter, and heed His commandments.
Nothing short of the throne of our hearts will satisfy the Lord
Jesus. In order to do this, the Holy Spirit casts down our carnal
imaginations, and every high thing that exalts itself against the
knowledge of God, and brings into captivity every thought to
the obedience of Christ (2 Corinthians 10:5), so that we freely
and gladly take His yoke upon us. This yoke is, as one of the Puritans said, "lined with love."

"No man can come to Me, except the Father which hath
sent Me draw him" (John 6:44). This "drawing" is accomplished
by the Spirit, first, in effectually enlightening the understanding;
second, by quickening the affections; third, by freeing the will
from the bondage of sin and inclining it toward God. By the
invincible workings of grace, the Spirit turns the bent of that
will, which before moved only toward sin and vanity, unto
Christ. "Thy people," said God unto the Mediator, "shall be
willing in the day of Thy power" (Psalm 110:3). Yet, though divine power is put forth upon a human object, the Spirit does
not infringe the will's prerogative of acting freely. He morally
persuades it. He subdues its sinful intractability. He overcomes
its prejudice, wins and draws it by the sweet attractions of grace.

Charles Spurgeon, in a sermon on John 6:37, said: "God
never treats man as though he were a brute. He does not drag
him with cart ropes. He treats men as men; and when He binds
them with cords, they are the cords of love and the bands of a
man. I may exercise power over another's will, and yet that other
man's will may be perfectly free, because the constraint is exer-

cised in a manner accordant with the laws of the human mind. If I show a man that a certain line of action is much for his advantage, he feels bound to follow it, but he is perfectly free in so doing. If man's will were subdued or chained by some physical process, if man's heart should, for instance, be taken from him and be turned round by a manual operation, that would be altogether inconsistent with human freedom, or indeed with human nature—and yet I think some few people imagine that I mean this when I talk of constraining influence and divine grace. I mean nothing of the kind. I mean that Jehovah Jesus knows how, by irresistible arguments addressed to the understanding, by mighty reasons appealing to the affections, and by the mysterious influence of His Holy Spirit operating upon all the powers and passions of the soul, so to subdue the whole man, that whereas it was once rebellious it becomes obedient; whereas it stood stoutly against the Most High, it throws down the weapons of its rebellion and cries, 'I yield! I yield! subdued by sovereign love, and by the enlightenment which Thou hast bestowed upon me, I yield myself to Thy will.'"

The perfect consistency between the freedom of a regenerated man's spiritual actions and the efficacious grace of God moving him thereto is seen in 2 Corinthians 8:16-17: "But thanks be to God, which put the same earnest care into the heart of Titus for you. For indeed he accepted the exhortation; but being more forward, of his own accord he went unto you." Titus was moved to that work by Paul's exhortation, and was "willing of his own accord" to engage therein; and yet it was God who put the same earnest care into the heart of Titus for them. God controls the inward feelings and acts of men without interfering either with their liberty or responsibility. The zeal of Titus was the spontaneous effusion of his own heart, and was an index to an element of his character; nevertheless, God wrought in him both to will and to do of His good pleasure.

No sinner savingly "comes to Christ," or truly receives Him into the heart, until the will freely consents (not merely "assents" in a theoretical way) to the severe and self-denying terms upon which He is presented in the gospel. No sinner is prepared to forsake all for Christ, take up the cross and follow Him in the path of universal obedience, until the heart genuinely esteems Him to be "the fairest among ten thousand." And this none will ever do before the understanding has been supernaturally enlightened and the affections supernaturally quickened. Obviously, none will espouse themselves with conjugal affections to that person whom they account is not the best that can be chosen. It is as the Spirit convicts us of our emptiness and shows us Christ's fullness, our guilt and His righteousness, our filthiness and the cleansing merits of His blood, our depravity and His holiness, that the heart is won and the resistance of the will is overcome.

The holy and spiritual truth of God finds nothing akin to itself in the unregenerate soul, but, instead, everything that is opposed to it (John 15:18; Romans 8:7). The demands of Christ are too humbling to our natural pride, too searching for the callous conscience, and too exacting for our fleshly desires. And a miracle of grace has to be wrought within us before this awful depravity of our nature, this dreadful state of affairs, is changed. That miracle of grace consists in overcoming the resistance that is made by indwelling sin, and creating desires and longings Christward; and then it is that the will cries:

> "Nay, but I yield, I yield,
> I can hold out no more;
> I sink, by dying love compell'd,

And own Thee Conqueror."

A beautiful illustration of this is found in Ruth 1:14–18. Naomi, a backslidden saint, is on the point of leaving the far country and (typically) returning to her father's house. Her two daughters-in-law wish to accompany her. Faithfully did Naomi bid them "count the cost" (Luke 14:28); instead of at once urging them to act on their first impulse, she pointed out the difficulties and trials to be encountered. This was too much for Orpah; her "goodness" (like that of the stony-ground hearers, and myriads of others) was only "as a morning cloud" and "as the early dew" it quickly went away (Hosea 6:4). In blessed contrast from this we read: "But Ruth clave unto her. . .[saying], 'Entreat me not to leave thee, or to return from following after thee; for whither thou goest, I will go; and where thou lodgest, I will lodge. Thy people shall be my people, and thy God my God."

What depth and loveliness of affection was here! What whole-hearted self-surrender! See Ruth freely and readily leaving her own country and kindred, tearing herself from every association of nature, turning a deaf ear to her mother-in-law's begging her to return to her gods (v. 15) and people. See her renouncing idolatry, and all that flesh holds dear, to be a worshipper and servant of the living God, counting all things but loss for the sake of His favor and salvation. And her future conduct proved her faith was genuine and her profession sincere. Ah, naught but a miraculous work of God in her soul can explain this. It was God working in her "both to will and to do of His good pleasure" (Philippians 2:13). He was drawing her with the bands of love; grace triumphed over the flesh. This is what every genuine conversion is—a complete surrender of the mind, heart and will to God and His Christ, so that there is a desire to "follow the Lamb whithersoever he goeth" (Revelation 14:4).

The relationship between our understanding being enlightened and the affections quickened by God and the resultant consent of the will is seen in Psalm 119:34: "Give me understanding, and I shall keep Thy law; yea, I shall observe it with my whole heart."

Again, to quote Spurgeon: "The sure result of regeneration, or the bestowal of understanding, is the devout reverence for the law, and a reverent keeping of it in the heart. The Spirit of God makes us to know the Lord and to understand somewhat of His love, wisdom, holiness, and majesty; and the result is that we honor the law and yield our hearts to the obedience of the faith. The understanding operates upon the affections; it convinces the heart of the beauty of the law, so that the soul loves it with all its powers; and then it reveals the majesty of the Lawgiver, and the whole nature bows before His supreme will. He alone obeys God who can say 'My Lord, I would serve Thee, and do it with all my heart'; and none can truly say this till they have received as a free grant the inward illumination of the Holy Spirit."

Before turning to my final section, a few words need to be added here upon 1 Peter 2:4-5: "To whom coming as unto a living stone. . .ye also, as lively stones, are built up a spiritual house." Has the sovereign grace of God inclined me to come unto Christ? Then it is my duty and interest to abide in Him (John 15:4), to abide in Him by a life of faith, and let His Spirit abide in me without grieving Him (Ephesians 4:30) or quenching His motions (1 Thessalonians 5:19). It is not enough that I once believed on Christ, I must live in and upon Him by faith daily (Galatians 2:20). It is in this way of continual coming to Christ that we are "built up a spiritual house." It is in this way the life of grace is maintained, until it issues in the life of glory. Faith is to be always receiving out of His fullness "grace for

grace" (John 1:16). There should be daily the renewed dedica-
tion of myself unto Him and the heart's occupation with Him.

13

Tests

Unto those who never savingly came to Christ, He will yet say, "Depart from Me, ye cursed, into everlasting fire, prepared for the devil and his angels." The contemplation of those awful words ought to almost freeze the very blood in our veins, searching our consciences and awing our hearts. But, alas, it is much to be feared that Satan will blunt their piercing force unto many of our readers by assuring them that they have already come to Christ, and telling them they are fools to doubt it for a moment. But, O dear friend, seeing that there is no less than your immortal soul at stake, that whether you spend eternity in heaven with the blessed or in hell with the cursed, hinges on whether or not you really and truly "come to Christ," will you not read the paragraphs that follow with double care?

1. How many rest on their sound doctrinal views of Christ. They believe firmly in His deity, His holy humanity, His perfect life, His vicarious death, His bodily resurrection, His ascension to God's right hand, His present intercession on high, and His second advent. So too did many of those to whom James addressed his epistle, but he reminded them that the "demons also believe and tremble" (James 2:19). O my reader, saving faith in Christ is very much more than assenting to the teachings of Scripture concerning Him; it is the giving up of the soul unto Him to be saved, to renounce all else, to yield fully unto Him.

2. How many mistake the absence of doubts for a proof they have savingly come to Christ. They take for granted that for which they have no clear evidence. But, reader, a man does not possess Christ by faith as he does money in a strongbox or title-deeds of land that are preserved by his lawyer, and that he never looks at once in a year. No, Christ is as bread that a man feeds upon, chews, and digests, that his stomach works upon continually, and by which he is nourished and strengthened (John 6:53). The empty professor feeds upon a good opinion of himself rather than upon Christ.

3. How many mistake the stirring of the emotions for the Spirit's quickening of the affections. If people weep under the preaching of the Word, superficial observers are greatly encouraged; and if they go forward to the "mourners' bench" and sob and wail over their sins, this is regarded as a sure sign that God has savingly convicted them. But a supernatural work of divine grace goes much deeper than that. Tears are but on the surface, and are a matter of temperamental constitution. Even in nature, some of those who feel things the most give the least outward sign of it. It is the weeping of the heart that God requires; it is a godly sorrow for sin that breaks its reigning power over the soul that evidences regeneration.

4. How many mistake a fear of the wrath to come for a hatred of sin. No one wants to go to hell. If the intellect is convinced of its reality, and the unspeakable awfulness of its torments are in a measure believed, then there may be great uneasiness of mind, fear of conscience, and anguish of heart over the prospect of suffering its eternal burnings. Those fears may last a considerable time, yea, their effects may never completely wear off. The subject of them may come under the ministry of a faithful servant of God, hear him describe the deep plowing of the Spirit's work, and conclude that he has been the subject of

them, yet have none of that love for Christ that manifests itself in a life, all the details of which seek to honor and glorify Him.

5. How many mistake a false peace for a true one. Let a person who has had awakened within him a natural dread of the lake of fire, whose own conscience has made him wretched, and the preaching he has heard terrify him yet more, then is he not (like a drowning man) ready to clutch at a straw. Let one of the false prophets of the day tell him that all he has to do is believe John 3:16 and salvation is his, and how eagerly will he—though unchanged in heart—drink in such "smooth things." Assured that nothing more is required than to firmly believe that God loves him and that Christ died for him, and his burden is gone; peace now fills him. Yes, and nineteen times out of twenty that "peace" is nothing but Satan's opiate, drugging his conscience and chloroforming him into hell. "There is no (true, spiritual) peace, saith my God, to the wicked," and unless the heart has been purified no man will see God (Matthew 5:8).

6. How many mistake self-confidence for spiritual assurance. It is natural for each of us to think well and hope well of ourselves, and to imagine with Haman, "I am the man whom the King delighteth to honor." Perhaps the reader is ready to say, "That is certainly not true of me! So far from having a high esteem, I regard myself as a worthless, sinful creature." Yes, and so deceitful is the human heart, and so ready is Satan to turn everything to his own advantage, these very lowly thoughts of self may be feasted on, and rested on to assure the heart that all is well with you. The apostate king Saul began by having a lowly estimate of himself (1 Samuel 9:21).

7. How many make a promise the sole ground of their faith, and look no further than the letter of it. Thus the Jews were deceived by the letter of the law, for they never saw the spiritual meaning of Moses' ministry. In like manner, multitudes are de-

ceived by the letter of such promises as Acts 16:31 and Romans 10:13, and do not look to Christ in them. They see that He is the jewel in the casket, but rest upon the superscription without, and never lay hold of the treasure within. But unless the person of Christ is apprehended, unless there is a real surrendering to His lordship, unless He is Himself received into the heart, then believing the letter of the promises will avail nothing.

The above paragraphs have been written in the hope that God may be pleased to arouse some empty professors out of their false security. But lest any of Christ's little ones stumble, I close with an excerpt from John Bunyan's *Come and Welcome to Jesus Christ*: "How shall we know that such men are coming to Christ? Answer: Do they cry out at sin, being burdened with it, as an exceedingly bitter thing? Do they fly from it, as from the face of a deadly serpent? Do they cry out of the insufficiency of their own righteousness, as to justification in the sight of God? Do they cry out after the Lord Jesus to save them? Do they see more worth and merit in one drop of Christ's blood to save them than in all the sins of the world to damn them? Are they tender of sinning against Jesus Christ? Do they favor Christ in this world, and do they leave all the world for His sake? And are they willing (God helping them) to run hazards for His name, for the love they bear to Him? Are His saints precious to them? If these things are so, these men are coming to Christ."

Part 4

Assurance

14

Assurances

By way of introduction, and in order to acquaint the reader with the particular angle of viewpoint from which I now approach our present theme, let it be pointed out that changing conditions in Christendom call for an ever-varying emphasis on different aspects of divine truth. At different periods the true servants of God have had to face widely different situations and meet errors of varied character. This has called for a campaign of offense and defense adapted to the exigencies of many situations. The weapons suited to one conflict were quite useless for another, fresh ones needing to be constantly drawn from the armory of Scripture.

At the close of that lengthy period known as the "dark ages" (though throughout it God never left Himself without a clear witness), when the Lord caused a flood of light to break forth upon Christendom, the Reformers were faced by the hoary errors of Romanism, among which was her insistence that none could be positively assured of his salvation till the hour of death was reached. This caused Luther and his contemporaries to deliver a positive message, seeking to stimulate confidence toward God and the laying hold of His sure promises. Yet it has to be acknowledged that there were times when their zeal carried them too far, leading to a position that could not be successfully defended from the Scriptures. Many of the Reformers insisted that assurance was an essential element in saving faith itself, and that unless a person knew he was "accepted in the Beloved" he was yet in his sins. Thus, in the revolt from Romanism, the Protestant pendulum swung too far to the opposite side.

In the great mercy of God the balance of truth was restored in the days of the Puritans. The principal doctrine that Luther and his fellows had emphasized so forcibly was justification by faith alone; but at the close of the sixteenth century, and in the early part of the seventeenth, such men as [William] Perkins, [Thomas] Gataker, [Robert] Rollock, and others, made prominent the collateral doctrine of sanctification by the Spirit. For the next fifty years the Church on earth was blessed with many men who were "mighty in the Scriptures," deeply taught of God, enabled by Him to maintain a well-rounded ministry. Such men as [Thomas] Goodwin, [John] Owen, [Stephen] Charnock, [John] Flavel, and [Richard] Sibbes, though living in troublous times and suffering fierce persecution, taught the Word more helpfully (in my judgment), and were more used of God, than any since the days of the apostles to the present hour.

The ministry of the Puritans was an exceedingly searching one. While magnifying the free grace of God in no uncertain terms, while teaching plainly that the satisfaction of Christ alone gave title to heaven, while emphatically repudiating all creature-merits, they nevertheless insisted that a supernatural and transforming work of the Spirit in the heart and life of the believer was indispensable to fit him for heaven. Professing believers were rigidly tested, and the results and fruits of faith were demanded before its presence was admitted. Self-examination was frequently insisted upon, and full details given as to how one might ascertain that he was a "new creature in Christ Jesus." Christians were constantly urged to "make their calling and election sure" by ascertaining that they had clear evidence of the same. While conditions were far from being perfect, yet there is

good reason to conclude that more deluded souls were undeceived and more hypocrites exposed than at any other period
since the first century A.D.

The eighteenth century witnessed a sad declension and departure from the faith. Worldly prosperity brought in spiritual
deterioration. As the Puritan leaders died off, none were raised
up to fill their places. Arminianism spread rapidly, followed by
Deism (Unitarianism) and other fatal errors. Worldliness en-
gulfed the churches, and lawlessness and wickedness were ram-
pant without. The gospel trumpet was almost silent, and the
remnant of God's people dwindled down to an insignificant
and helpless handful. But where sin abounded, grace did much
more abound. Again the light of God shone forth powerfully in
the darkness, [George] Whitefield, [William] Romaine, [John]
Gill, [James] Hervey, and others, being raised up by God to revive His saints and convert many sinners to Christ. The main
emphasis of their preaching and teaching was upon the sovereign grace of God as exhibited in the everlasting covenant, the
certain efficacy of Christ's atonement unto all for whom it was
made, and the work of the Spirit in regeneration.

Under the God-given revivals of the latter part of the eighteenth century, the great doctrines of the Christian faith occupied the most prominent place. In order that the balance of
truth might be preserved during the next two or three generations it became necessary for the servants of God to emphasize
the experimental side of things. Intellectual orthodoxy qualifies
none for heaven; there must be a moral and spiritual transfor-
mation, a miracle of grace wrought within the soul, that begins
at regeneration and is carried on by sanctification. During that
period doctrinal exposition receded more and more into the
background, and the practical application of the Word to the
heart and life was the characteristic feature in orthodox circles.

This called for serious self-examination, and that, in many cases, resulted in doubtings and despondency. Where a due balance is not preserved by preachers and teachers between the objective and subjective sides of the truth, where the latter preponderates, either a species of mysticism or a lack of assurance ensues.

The second half of last century found many circles of professing Christians on the borders of the Slough of Despond. In many companies the full assurance of salvation was looked upon as a species of fanaticism or as carnal presumption. Unduly occupied with themselves, ill-instructed upon the "two natures" in the Christian, thousands of poor souls regarded doubts and fears, sighs and groans, as the highest evidence of a regenerate state; but those being mixed with worldly and fleshly lusts, the subjects were afraid to affirm they were children of God. To meet this situation many ill-trained evangelists and teachers sought to direct attention to Christ and His "finished work," and to get their hearers' confidence placed upon the bare Word of God. While one evil was corrected another was committed; while the letter of Scripture was honored, the work of the Spirit was (unwittingly) dishonored. Supposing they had a remedy that was sure to work in all cases alike, a superficial work resulted, the aftermath of which we are now reaping. Thousands of souls who give no evidence of being born again are quite confident that Christ has saved them.

From the brief outline presented above, it will be seen that the pendulum has swung from one side to the other. Man is a creature of extremes, and nothing but the grace of God can enable any of us to steer a middle path. A careful study of the course of religious history also reveals the fact that the servants of God have been obliged, from time to time, to vary their note of emphasis. This is one meaning of that expression, "and be established in the present truth" (2 Peter 1:12), namely that particular aspect or line of truth that is most needful at any given time. Instead of gaining ground, the Puritans had lost it had they merely echoed what the Reformers had taught. It was not that Owen contradicted Luther, rather he supplemented him. Where particular stress has been laid on the counsels of sovereign grace and the imputed righteousness of Christ, this needs to be followed by attention being drawn to the work of the Spirit within the saints. In like manner, where much ministry has been given on the Christian's state, there is a need for a clear exposition of his standing before God.

It is truly deplorable that so few have recognized the need for applying the principle that has just been mentioned. So many, having a zeal that is not tempered by knowledge, suppose that because some honored servant of God in the past was granted much success through his dwelling so largely upon one particular line of truth that they will have equal success, provided they imitate him. But circumstances alter cases. The different states through which the professing Church passes calls for different ministry. There is such a thing as "a word spoken in due season" (Proverbs 15:23). Oh, that it may please God to open the eyes of many to see what is most "seasonable" for the degenerate times in which our lot is cast, and grant them spiritual discernment to recognize that even many portions of divine truth may prove highly injurious to souls if given to them out of season.

We recognize this fact easily enough in connection with material things, why are we so slow to do so when it concerns spiritual things? Meats and nuts are nutritious, but who would think of feeding an infant upon them? So too sickness of the body calls for a change of diet. The same is true of the soul. To make this clearer, let me select one or two extreme cases. The truth of eternal punishment should be faithfully preached by every servant of God, but would a broken-hearted woman who had just lost her husband or child be a suitable audience? The glory and bliss of the heavenly state is a precious theme, but would it be fitting to present it unto a professing Christian who was intoxicated? The eternal security of the saints is clearly revealed in Holy Writ, but does that justify me in pressing it on the attention of a backslidden child of God?

My introduction has been a lengthy one, yet I deemed it necessary to pave the way for what follows. The servant of God is facing today a dreadfully serious and solemn situation. Much that is dearest of all to his heart he has largely to be silent upon. If he is to faithfully deal with souls, he must address himself to the condition they are in. Unless he is much upon his guard, unless he constantly seeks wisdom and guidance from above, he is likely to make bad matters worse. On every side are people full of assurance, certain that they are journeying to heaven, yet their daily lives show plainly that they are deceived, and that their assurance is only a fleshly one. Thousands are, to use their own words, "resting on John 3:16," or John 5:24, and have not the slightest doubt they will spend eternity with Christ. Nevertheless, it is the bound duty of every real servant of God to tell the great majority of them that they are woefully deluded by Satan. Oh, that it may please God to give us the ear and serious attention of some of them.

Some time ago I read of an incident that, as nearly as I recall, was as follows. Nearly one hundred years since, conditions in England were similar to what they have recently been in this country. Banks were failing and people were panic-stricken. One man who had lost confidence in the banks drew out all his money in five-pound notes, and then got a friend to change them into gold. Conditions grew worse, other banks failed, and some of this man's friends told him they had lost their all. With much confidence he informed them that he had drawn out his money, had changed it into gold, and that this was secretly hidden where no one would find it, so that he was perfectly safe. A little later, when needing to buy some things, he went to his secret hoard and took out five golden sovereigns. He went from one shop to another, but none would accept them— they were bad ones. Thoroughly alarmed, he went to his hidden money, only to find that it was all counterfeit coin!

Now, dear reader, you too may be quite sure that your faith in Christ is true "gold," and yet, after all, be mistaken. The danger of this is not to be fancied, but real. The human heart is dreadfully deceitful (Jeremiah 17:9). God's Word plainly warns us that, "There is a generation that are pure in their own eyes, and yet is not washed from their filthiness" (Proverbs 30:12). If you ask (oh, that you may, in deep earnestness and sincerity), "How can I be sure that my faith is a genuine and saving one?" The answer is, test it. Make certain that it is the "faith of God's elect" (Titus 1:1). Ascertain whether or not your faith is accompanied with those fruits that are inseparable from a God-given and Spirit-wrought faith.

Probably many are ready to say, "There is no need for me to be put to any such trouble. I know that my faith is a saving one, for I am resting on the finished work of Christ." But, dear friend, it is foolish to talk like that. God Himself bids His people to make their "calling and election sure" (2 Peter 1:10). Is that a needless exhortation? Oh, do not pit your vain confidence against divine wisdom. It is Satan who is striving so hard to keep many from this very task, lest they discover that their house is built on the sand. There is hope for one who discovers his illusion, but there is none for those who go on believing the devil's lie, and rest content with the very real but false peace that he gives to so many of his poor victims.

God Himself has supplied us with tests, and we are mad if we do not avail ourselves of them, and honestly measure ourselves by them. "These things have I written unto you that believe on the name of the Son of God, that ye may know that ye have eternal life, and that ye may believe (more intelligently) on the name of the Son of God" (1 John 5:13). The Holy Spirit Himself moved one of His servants to write a whole epistle to instruct us how we might know whether or not we have eternal life. Does that look as though the question may be determined and settled as easily as so many present-day preachers and writers represent it? If nothing more than a firm persuasion of the truth of John 3:16 or 5:24 is needed to assure me of my salvation, then why did God give a whole epistle to instruct us on this subject?

Let the really concerned soul read slowly and thoughtfully through this first epistle of John, and let him duly observe that not once in its five chapters are we told, "We know that we have passed from death unto life because we are resting on the finished work of Christ." The total absence of such a statement ought, surely, to convince us that something must be radically wrong with so much of the popular teaching of the day on this subject. But not only is there no such declaration made in this epistle, the very first passage that contains the familiar "we know" is quite the reverse of what is now being so widely advocated as the ground of Christian assurance. "And hereby we do know that we know Him, if we keep His commandments" (1 John 2:3). Is not that plain enough? A godly life is the first proof that I am a child of God.

But let us observe the solemn declaration that immediately follows. "He that saith, 'I know Him,' and keepeth not his commandments, is a liar, and the truth is not in him" (1 John 2:4). Do these words anger you? I trust not; they are God's words, not mine. Do you refuse to read any more of this article? That would be a bad sign; an honest heart does not fear the light. A sincere soul is willing to be searched by the truth. If you are unable to endure now the feeble probing of one of His servants, how will it fare in a soon-coming day when the Lord Himself shall search you through and through? O dear friend, give your poor soul a fair chance, be willing to ascertain whether your faith is real wheat, or only chaff. If it proves to be the latter, there is still time for you to humble yourself before God and cry unto Him to give you saving faith. But in that day it will be too late!

"He that saith, 'I know Him,' and keepeth not his commandments, is a liar, and the truth is not in him" (1 John 2:4). How plain and pointed is this language! How awful is its clear intimation! Do you not see, dear reader, this verse plainly implies that there are those who claim to know Christ and yet are liars. The father of lies has deceived them, and he is doing everything in his power to keep them from being undeceived. That is why the unregenerate reader finds this article so unpalatable, and wishes to turn from it. Oh, resist this inclination, I beseech you. God has given us this very verse by which we may measure ourselves, and discover whether or not our "assurance of salvation" will stand the test of His Holy Word. Then do not act like the silly ostrich, that buries his head in the sand rather than face his danger.

Let me quote one more verse from this first "we know" passage in John's epistle: "But whoso keepeth His Word, in him verily is the love of God perfected; hereby know we that we are in Him" (1 John 2:5). This stands in sharp contrast from the preceding verse. The apostle was here moved to set before us some clear scriptural evidences of spiritual faith and love, that constitute the vital difference between sheep and goats. In verse

4 it is the empty professor who says, "I know Christ as my personal Savior." He has a theoretical, but not a vital knowledge of Him. He boasts that he is resting on Christ's finished work, and is confident that he is saved, but does not keep His commandments. He is still a self-pleaser. Like Solomon's sluggard, he is "wiser in his own conceit than seven men that can render a reason" (Proverbs 26:16). He talks boldly, but walks carelessly.

In verse 5 it is the genuine Christian who is in view. He does not say, "I know Him," instead he proves it. The apostle is not here presenting Christ as the immediate Object of faith, but is describing him who has savingly fled to the Lord for refuge, and this by the effects produced. In him Christ's Word is everything, his food, his constant meditation, his chart. He "keeps" it, in memory, in heart, and in action. Christ's commandments occupy his thoughts and prayers as much as do His promises. That Word working in him subdues his carnal desires, feeds his graces, and draws them into real exercise and act. That Word has such a place in his heart and mind that he cannot but give proof of the same in his talk and walk. In this way the love of God is perfected; the family likeness is plainly stamped upon him; all can see to which "father" he belongs—contrast John 8:44.

"Whoso keepeth His Word. . .hereby (in this way) know we that we are in Him." Keep His Word perfectly? No, but actually, characteristically, in deep desire and honest effort to do so. Yes, regeneration is that miracle of divine grace wrought in the soul that enlists the affections God-ward, that brings the human will into subjection to the divine, and that produces a real and radical change in the life. That change is from worldliness to godliness, from disobedience to obedience. At the new birth, the love of God is shed abroad in the heart by the Holy Spirit, and that love is manifested in a dominating longing and sincere purpose to please in all things the One who has plucked me as a brand from the burning. There is a greater difference between the genuine Christian and the deceived, professing Christian than there is between a living man and a corpse. None need remain in doubt if they will honestly measure themselves by the Holy Word of God.

There is only space for us to consider one other Scripture in this opening article, namely the Parable of the Sower. Why did the Lord Jesus give us that parable? Why, but to stir me up to serious inquiry and diligent examination so as to discover which kind of a "hearer" I am. In that parable, Christ likened those who hear the Word unto various sorts of ground upon which the seed falls. He divided them into four different classes. Three out of the four brought no fruit to perfection. That is exceedingly solemn and searching. In one case, the devil catches away the good seed out of the heart (Luke 8:12). In another case, they "for a while believe, and in time of temptation fall away" (Luke 8:13). In another case, they are "choked with cares and riches and pleasures of this life" (Luke 8:14). Are you, my reader, described in one of these? Do not ignore this question, I beg you. Face it honestly, and make sure which of the various soils represents your heart.

But there are some "good ground" hearers. And how are they to be identified? What did the infallible Son of God say of them? How did He describe them? Did He say that, "On the good ground are they who rest on the Word of God, and do not doubt His promises, are thoroughly persuaded they are saved, and yet go on living the same kind of life as previously"? No, He did not. Instead, He declared, "But that on the good ground are they which in an honest and good heart, having heard the Word, keep it, and bring forth fruit with patience" (Luke 8:15). Ah, dear readers, the test is fruit—not knowledge, not boastings, not orthodoxy, not joy, but fruit—and such "fruit" as mere nature cannot produce. It is the fruit of the Vine, namely likeness to Christ, being conformed to His image. May the Holy Spirit search each one of us.

Can true believers be infallibly assured that they are in the state of grace, and that they shall persevere therein unto salvation? I answer, such as truly believe in Christ, and endeavor to walk in all good conscience before Him (1 John 2:3), may, without extraordinary revelation, by faith grounded upon the truth of God's promises, and by the Spirit enabling them to discern in themselves those graces to which the promises of life are made (1 John 3:14, 18, 19, 21, 24; Hebrews 6:11-12), and bearing witness with their spirits that they are the children of God (Romans 8:16), be infallibly assured that they are in the state of grace and shall persevere therein unto salvation (1 John 5:13; 2 Timothy 1:12).

"Assurance is the believer's full conviction that, through the work of Christ alone, received by faith, he is in possession of a salvation in which he will be eternally kept. And this assurance rests only upon the Scripture promises to him who believes."

The careful reader will perceive a considerable difference of doctrine in the two paragraphs given above. The former is the product of the Puritans, the latter is a fair sample of what the boasted enlightenment of the twentieth century has brought forth. The one is extracted from the *Westminster Confession of Faith* (the doctrinal statement of the Presbyterians), the other is taken from the *Scofield Bible*. In the one, the balance of truth is helpfully preserved; in the second, the work and witness of the Holy Spirit is altogether ignored. This example is only one out of scores I could cite, which sadly illustrates how far we have gone backward. The answer given by the Puritans is calculated to lead to heart searchings; the definition (if such it may be called) of the popular dispensationalist is likely to bolster up the deluded. This brings us to consider, more definitely, the nature of assurance.

15

The Nature of Assurance

Let us begin by asking the question, Assurance of what? That the Holy Scriptures are the inspired and infallible Word of God? No, that is not our subject. Assured that salvation is by grace alone? No, for neither is that our immediate theme. Rather, the assurance that I am no longer in a state of nature, but in a state of grace; and this, not as a mere conjectural persuasion, but as resting on sure evidence. It is a well-authenticated realization that not only has my mind been enlightened concerning the great truths of God's Word, but that a supernatural work has been wrought in my soul that has made me a new creature in Christ Jesus. A scriptural assurance of salvation is that knowledge which the Holy Spirit imparts to the heart through the Scriptures, that my "faith" is not a natural one, but "the faith of God's elect" (Titus 1:1), that my love for Christ is sincere and not fictitious, that my daily walk is that of a regenerate man.

The assurance of the saints is, as the Westminster divines said, "by the Spirit enabling them to discern in themselves those graces to which the promises of life are made." Let me seek to amplify that statement. At the commencement of Matthew 5 we find the Lord Jesus pronouncing blessed a certain class of people. They are not named as "believers" or "saints," but instead are described by their characters; and it is only by comparing ourselves and others with the description that the Lord Jesus there gave that we are enabled to identify such. First, He said, "Blessed are the poor in spirit." To be "poor in spirit" is to have a feeling sense that in me, that is, in my flesh, "there dwelleth no good thing" (Romans 7:18). It is the realization that I am utterly destitute of anything and everything that could commend me favorably to God's notice. It is to recognize that I am spiritually bankrupt. It is the consciousness even now (not years ago, when I was first awakened) that I am without strength and wisdom, and that I am a helpless creature, completely dependent upon the grace and mercy of God. To be "poor in spirit" is the opposite of Laodiceanism, which consists of self-complacency and self-sufficiency, imagining I am "rich, and in need of nothing."

"Blessed are they that mourn." It is one thing to believe the theory that I am spiritually a poverty-stricken pauper; it is quite another to have an acute sense of it in my soul. Where the latter exists, there are deep exercises of heart that evoke the bitter cry, "my leanness, my leanness, woe unto me!" (Isaiah 24:16). There is deep anguish that there is so little growth in grace, so little fruit to God's glory, such a wretched return made for His abounding goodness unto me. This is accompanied by an ever-deepening discovery of the depths of corruption that is still within me. The soul finds that when it would do good, evil is present with him (Romans 7:21). It is grieved by the motions of unbelief, the swellings of pride, the surging of rebellion against God. Instead of peace, there is war within; instead of realizing his holy aspirations, the blessed one is daily defeated; until the stricken heart cries out, "O wretched man that I am! Who shall deliver me from the body of this death?" (Romans 7:24).

"Blessed are the meek." Meekness is yieldedness. It is the opposite of self-will. Meekness is pliability and meltedness of heart, which makes me submissive and responsive to God's will.

Now observe, dear reader, these first three marks of the "blessed" consist not in outward actions, but of inward graces; not in showy deeds, but in states of soul. Note too that they are far from being characteristics that will render their possessor pleasing and popular to the world. He who feels himself to be a spiritual pauper will not be welcomed by the wealthy Laodiceans. He who daily mourns for his leanness, his barrenness, and his sinfulness, will not be courted by the self-righteous. He who is truly meek will not be sought after by the self-assertive. No, he will be scorned by the Pharisees and looked upon with contempt by those who boast they are "out of Romans 7 and living in Romans 8." These lovely graces, which are of great price in the sight of God, are despised by the bloated professors of the day.

We must not now review the additional marks of the "blessed" named by the Redeemer at the beginning of His precious Sermon on the Mount, but at one other one we will just glance. "Blessed are they which are persecuted for righteousness' sake.. Blessed are ye when men shall revile you. . .for My sake" (Matthew 5:10–11). Observe that this antagonism is not evoked by wrongdoing, or by a well-grounded offence. They who are morose, selfish, haughty, evil speakers, cruel, have no right to shelter behind this beatitude when people retaliate against them. No, it is where Christ-likeness of character and conduct is assailed; where practical godliness condemns the worldly ways of empty professors, that fires their enmity; where humble but vital piety cannot be tolerated by those who are destitute of the same. "Blessed," said Christ, "are the spiritual, whom the carnal hate, the gentle sheep whom the dogs snap at."

Now, dear reader, seek grace to honestly measure yourself by these criteria. Do such heavenly graces adorn your soul? Are these marks of those whom the Son of God pronounced "blessed" stamped upon your character? Are you truly "poor in spirit"? I say "truly," for it is easy to adopt expressions and call ourselves names—if you are offended when someone else applies them to you, it shows you do not mean what you say. Do you "mourn" over your lack of conformity to Christ, the feebleness of your faith, the coldness of your love? Are you "meek"? Has your will been broken and your heart made submissive to God? Do you hunger and thirst after righteousness? Do you use the means of grace? Do your searching of the Scriptures, your prayers, evince it? Are you "merciful," or censorious and harsh? Are you "pure in heart," grieved when an impure imagination assails? If not, you have no right to regard yourself as "blessed"; instead you are under the curse of a holy and sin-hating God.

It is not, are these spiritual graces fully developed within you (they never are in this life), but are they truly present at all? It is not, are you completely emptied of self, but is it your sincere desire and earnest prayer to be so. It is not, do you "mourn" as deeply as you ought over indwelling sin and its activities, but have you felt at all "the plague" of your own heart (1 Kings 8:38)? It is not, is your meekness all that can be desired, but is there unmistakable proof that the root of it has actually been communicated to your soul? There is a growth: "first the blade, then the ear, then the full corn in the ear." But that which has no existence can have no growth. Has the "seed" (1 Peter 1:23) of grace been planted in your heart? That is the point which each of us is called upon to determine—not to assume, or take for granted, but to make "sure" (2 Peter 1:10) of. And this is done when we faithfully examine our hearts to discover whether or not there is in them those spiritual graces to which the promises of God are addressed.

While gospel assurance is the opposite of carnal presumption and of unbelieving doubts, yet it is far from being opposed to thorough self-examination. But, alas, so many have been taught, and by men highly reputed for their orthodoxy, that if it is not actually wrong, it is highly injurious for a Christian to look within. There is a balance of truth to be observed here, as everywhere. That one might become too introspective is readily granted, but that a Christian is never to search his own heart, test his faith, scrutinize his motives, and make sure that he has the "root of the matter" within him (Job 19:28), is contradicted by many plain Scriptures. Regeneration is a work that God performs within us (Philippians 1:6); and as eternal destiny hinges on the same, it behooves every serious soul to take the utmost pains and ascertain whether or not this miracle of grace has been wrought within him. When Paul stood in doubt of the state of the Galatians, he said, "My little children, of whom I travail in birth again until Christ be formed in you" (4:19). So to the Colossians he wrote, "Christ in you, the hope of glory" (1:27).

"For everyone that doeth evil hateth the light, neither cometh to the light, lest his deeds should be reproved. But he that doeth truth cometh to the light, that his deeds may be made manifest, that they are wrought in (or 'by') God" (John 3:20-21). Here is one of the vital differences between the unregenerate and the regenerate, the unbelieving and the believing. Unbelief is far more than an error of judgment, or speculative mistake into which an honest mind may fall; it proceeds from heart-enmity against God. The natural man, while left to himself, hates the searching light of God (verse 19), fearful lest it should disquiet the conscience, expose the fallacy of his presumptuous confidence, and shatter his false peace. But it is the very reverse with him who has been given an honest and good heart. He who acts sincerely and conscientiously, desiring to know and do the whole will of God without reserve, welcomes the light.

The genuine Christian believes what Scripture says concerning the natural heart, namely that it is "deceitful above all things" (Jeremiah 17:9), and the surest proof that he does believe this solemn fact is that he is deeply concerned lest "a deceived heart hath turned him aside" (Isaiah 44:20), and caused him to believe that all is well with his soul, when in reality he is yet "in the gall of bitterness, and the bond of iniquity." He believes what God's Word says about Satan, the great deluder, and trembles lest, after all, the devil has beguiled him with a false peace. Such a possibility, such a likelihood, occasions him much exercise of soul. Like David of old (and every other genuine saint), he communes with his own heart (Psalm 4:4), and his spirit makes diligent search (Psalm 77:6). He turns to the light of Holy Writ, anxious to have his character and conduct scrutinized by the same, desiring to have his deeds made manifest, as to whether they proceed from self-love or real love to God.

It is not that I am here seeking to foster any confidence in self; rather I desire to promote real confidence toward God. It is one thing to make sure that I love God, and it is quite another for me to find satisfaction in that love. The self-examination that the Scriptures enjoin (in 1 Corinthians 11:28, for example) is not for the purpose of finding something within to make me more acceptable to God, nor as a ground of my justification before Him; but is with the object of discovering whether Christ is being formed in me. There are two extremes to be guarded against: such an undue occupation with the work of the Spirit within that the heart is taken off from the work of Christ for His people, and such a one-sided emphasis upon the imputed righteousness of Christ that the righteousness imparted by the Spirit is ignored and disparaged. It is impossible that the Third

Person of the Trinity should take up His abode within a soul without effecting a radical change within him—and it is this that I need to make sure of. It is the Spirit's work within the heart that is the only infallible proof of salvation.

It is perfectly true that as I look within and seek to faithfully examine my heart in the light of Scripture, that the work of the Spirit is not all I shall discover there. No, indeed; much corruption still remains. The genuine Christian finds clear evidence of two natures, two contrary principles at work within him. This is brought out plainly, not only in Romans 7 and Galatians 5:17, but strikingly too in the Song of Solomon. "What will ye see in the Shulamite? As it were the company of two armies" (6:13). Hence it is that in her present state, the bride says, "I am black, but comely, O ye daughters of Jerusalem, as the tents of Kedar, as the curtains of Solomon" (1:5). And again, "I sleep, but my heart waketh" (5:2)—strange language to the natural man, but quite intelligible to the spiritual. And therefore is it also that the renewed soul so often finds suited to his case the prayer of Mark 9:24: "Lord, I believe; help Thou mine unbelief."

It is because the real Christian finds within himself so much that is conflicting that it is difficult for him to be sure of his actual state. And therefore he cries, "Examine me, O Lord, and prove me; try my reins and my heart" (Psalm 26:2). They who are filled with a carnal assurance, a fleshly confidence, a vain presumption, feel no need for asking the Lord to "prove" them. So completely has Satan deceived them that they imagine it would be an act of unbelief so to do. Poor souls, they "call evil good, and good evil"; they "put darkness for light, and light for darkness" (Isaiah 5:20). One of the surest marks of regeneration is that the soul frequently cries "Search me, O God, and know my heart. Try me, and know my thoughts, and see if there be any wicked way in me, and lead me in the way everlasting" (Psalm 139:23-24).

Perhaps some of my readers are still ready to say, "I do not see that there needs to be so much difficulty in ascertaining whether one is in a lost or saved condition. I am resting upon John 5:24, and that is sufficient for me." But allow ne to point out, dear friend, that John 5:24 is not a promise that Christ gave to an individual disciple, but, instead, a doctrinal declaration that He made in the hearing of a mixed multitude. If the objector replies, "I believe that verse does contain a promise, and I am going to hold fast to it," then may I lovingly ask, Are you sure that it belongs to you? That John 5:24 contains a precious promise I gladly acknowledge; but to whom is it made?

Let us examine it: "Verily, verily, I say unto you, He that heareth My word, and believeth on Him that sent Me, hath everlasting life, and shall not come into condemnation, but is passed from death unto life."

That promise is given to a definitely defined character, namely "He that heareth My word." Now, dear reader, can it be truthfully said that you are one that "heareth" His Word? Are you sure? Do not be misled by the mere sound of words. The reference here is not to the hearing of the outward ear, but to the response of the heart. In the days that He sojourned on earth, there were many of whom the Lord Jesus had to say that "hearing (with the outward ear), they hear not" with the heart (Matthew 13:13). So it is still. To "hear" spiritually, to "hear" savingly, is to heed (Matthew 18:15), is to obey (Matthew 17:5; John 10:27; Hebrews 3:7). Ah, are you obedient? Have you searched the Scriptures diligently in order to discover His commandments—and that, not to satisfy an idle curiosity, but desiring to put them into practice? Do you love His commandments? Are you actually doing them? Not once or twice, but regularly, as the main tenor of your life—for note it is not "hear" but "heareth."

Does someone object, "All of this is getting away from the simplicity of Christ. You are taking us from the Word, and seeking to get us occupied with ourselves."

Well, does not Scripture say, "Take heed unto thyself" (1 Timothy 4:16)?

But it may be answered, "There cannot be any certainty while we are occupied with our wretched selves. I prefer to abide by the written Word." To this I have no objection at all: what I am here pressing is the vital necessity of making sure that the portions of the Word you cite or are resting upon fairly and squarely belong to you. The reader may refer me to "Believe on the Lord Jesus Christ, and thou shalt be saved" (Acts 16:31) and ask, "Is not that plain enough?" But have you ever noted, dear friend, to whom the apostles addressed those words, and all the attendant circumstances?

It was neither to a promiscuous crowd, nor to a careless and unconcerned soul, that the apostles said, "Believe on the Lord Jesus Christ and thou shalt be saved." Rather it was to an awakened, deeply exercised, penitent soul who had taken his place in the dust, and in deepest anguish cried, "What must I do to be saved?" However, what is the use you are making of Acts 16:31? You answer, "This: those words are divinely simple, I believe in Christ, and therefore I am saved. God says so, and the devil cannot shake me." Possibly he is not at all anxious to; he may be well content for you to retain a carnal confidence. But observe, dear friend, the apostles did not tell the stricken jailor to "believe on Jesus" nor "believe in Christ," but to "believe on the Lord Jesus Christ."

What does it mean to savingly "believe"? I have sought to answer this question at length in my previous articles on "Saving

Faith." But let me now give a brief reply. John 1:12 makes it clear that to "believe" is to "receive," to receive "Christ Jesus the Lord" (Colossians 2:6). Christ is the Savior of none until He is welcomed as Lord. The immediate context shows plainly the particular character in which Christ is there viewed: "He came unto His own" (John 1:11). He was their rightful Owner because He was their Lord. But "His own received Him not." No, they declared, "We will not have this man to reign over us" (Luke 19:14). Ah, dear friend, this is searching. Have you received "the Lord Jesus Christ"? I do not ask, "Are you resting on His finished work," but have you bowed to His scepter and owned His authority in a practical way? Have you disowned your own sinful lordship? If not, you certainly have not "believed on the Lord Jesus Christ," and therefore the promise of Acts 16:31 does not belong to you.

"Now if any man have not the Spirit of Christ, he is none of his" (Romans 8:9). This is just as much a part of God's Word as is Acts 16:31. Why do we not hear it quoted as frequently! And how can anyone know that he is indwelt by the Spirit of Christ? Only by discovering within him the fruits of His regenerating and sanctifying grace. Not that either these "fruits" or the "good works" of the Christian are in any wise or to any degree meritorious. No, no; they only serve as the evidence of his divine sonship.

16

The Basis for Assurance

The task that these articles set before us is by no means easily executed. On the one hand, I wish to be kept from taking the children's bread and casting it to the dogs; on the other, it is my earnest prayer that we may be delivered from casting a stumbling-block before any of God's little ones. That which occasions my difficulty is the desire to expose an empty profession, and to be used of God in writing that which, under His free Spirit, may be used in removing the scales from the eyes of those who, though unregenerate, are resting with carnal confidence on some of the divine promises given to those who are in Christ; for while a sinner is out of Christ none of the promises belong to him (see 2 Corinthians 1:20). Notwithstanding, it behooves me to seek wisdom from above so that I may write in such a way that any of Christ's who are yet not established in the faith may not draw the conclusion that they are still dead in trespasses and sins.

Having before us the twofold objective named above, let me ask the question, Is a simple faith in Christ sufficient to save a soul for time and eternity? At the risk of some readers turning away from this article and refusing to read further, I unhesitatingly answer, No, it is not. The Lord Jesus Himself declared, "Except ye repent, ye shall all likewise perish" (Luke 13:3). Repentance is just as essential to salvation as is believing. Again, we read, "Wilt thou know, O vain man, that faith without works is

dead" (James 2:20). A "simple faith" that remains alone, a faith
that does not purify the heart (Acts 15:9), work by love (Galatians 5:6), and overcome the world (1 John 5:4), will save no-
body.

Much confusion has been caused in many quarters through
failure to define clearly what it is from which the sinner needs
saving. Only too often the thought of many minds is restricted
to hell. But that is a very inadequate conception, and often
proves most misleading. The only thing that can ever take any
creature to hell is sin that is unrepented of and unforgiven. Now
on the very first page of the New Testament the Holy Spirit has
particularly recorded it that the incarnate Son of God was
named "Jesus" because "He shall save His people from their
sins" (Matthew 1:21). Why is it that that which God has placed
at the forefront is relegated to the rear by most of modern evangelists? To ask a person if he has been saved from hell is much
more ambiguous than to inquire if he has been saved from his
sins.

Let me attempt to enlarge on this a little, for thousands of
professing Christians in these days have but the vaguest idea of
what it means to be saved from sin. First, it signifies to be saved
from the love of sin. The heart of the natural man is wedded to
everything that is opposed to God. He may not acknowledge it,
he may not be conscious of it, yet such is the fact nevertheless.
Having been shapen in iniquity and conceived in sin (Psalm
51:5), man cannot but be enamored with that which is now part
and parcel of his very being. When the Lord Jesus explained
why condemnation rests upon the unsaved, He declared, "men
loved darkness rather than light" (John 3:19). Nothing but a supernatural change of heart can deliver any from this dreadful
state. Only an omnipotent Redeemer can bring us to "abhor"
(Job 42:6) ourselves and loath iniquity. This He does when He

saves a soul, for "the fear of the Lord is to hate evil" (Proverbs 8:13).

Second, to be saved from our sins is to be delivered from the allowance of them. It is the unvarying tendency of the natural heart to excuse evildoing, to extenuate and gloss it over. At the beginning, Adam declined to acknowledge his guilt and sought to throw the blame upon his wife. It was the same with Eve: instead of honestly acknowledging her wickedness, she attempted to place the onus on the serpent. But how different is the regenerated person's attitude toward sin! "For that which I do, I allow not" (Romans 7:15). Paul committed sin, but he did not approve of it, still less did he seek to vindicate, it. He disclaimed all friendliness toward it. Nay, more, the real Christian repents of his wrongdoing, confesses it to God, mourns over it, and prays earnestly to be kept from a repetition of the same. Pride, coldness, slothfulness, he hates; yet day by day he finds them reasserting their power over him; and nightly he returns to the Fountain which has been opened "for sin and for uncleanness" (Zechariah 13:1) that he may be cleansed. The true Christian desires to render perfect obedience to God, and cannot rest satisfied with anything short of it; and instead of palliating his failures, he mourns over them.

Third, to be saved from our sins is to be delivered from the reigning power or mastery of them. Sin still indwells the Christian, tempts, annoys, wounds, and daily trips him up. "In many things we offend all" (James 3:2). Nevertheless, sin is not the complete master of the Christian, for he resists and fights against it. While far from being completely successful in his fight, yet, on the other hand, there is a vast difference between him and the helpless slaves of Satan. His repenting, his prayers, his aspirations after holiness, his pressing forward unto the mark set before him, all witness to the fact that sin does not

have "dominion" over (Romans 6:14) him. Undoubtedly there
are great differences of attainment among God's children. In
His high sovereignty, God grants more grace unto one than to
another. Some of His children are far more plagued by constitu-
tional sins than others. Some who are very largely delivered
from outward transgressions are yet made to groan over inward
ones. Some who are largely kept from sins of commission have
yet to bewail sins of omission. Yet sin is no longer complete
master over any who belong to the household of faith.

The last sentence may perhaps discourage some who have a
sensitive conscience. He who is really honest with himself and
has had his eyes opened in some degree to see the awful sinfulness of self, and who is becoming more and more acquainted
with that sink of iniquity, that mass of corruption that still indwells him, often feels that sin more completely rules him now
than ever it did before. When he longs to trust God with all his
heart, unbelief seems to paralyze him. When he wishes to be
completely surrendered to God's blessed will, murmurings and
rebellion surge within him. When he would spend an hour in
meditating on the things of God, evil imaginations harass him.
When he desires to be more humble, pride seeks to fill him.
When he would pray, his mind wanders. The more he fights
against these sins, the further off victory seems to be. To him it
appears that sin is very much the master of him, and Satan tells
him that his profession is vain. What shall we say to such a dear
soul who is deeply exercised over this problem? Two things.

First, the very fact that you are conscious of these sins, and
are so much concerned over your failure to overcome them, is a
healthy sign. It is the blind who cannot see; it is the dead who
do not feel—true alike naturally and spiritually. Only they who
have been quickened into newness of life are capable of real sorrow for sin. Moreover, such experiences as I have mentioned

above evidence a spiritual growth, a growth in the knowledge of self. As the wise man tells us, "He that increaseth knowledge increaseth sorrow" (Ecclesiastes 1:18). In God's light we see light (Psalm 36:9). The more the Holy Spirit reveals to me the high claims of God's holiness, the more I discover how far short I come of meeting them. Let the midday sun shine into a darkened room, and dust and dirt that before were invisible are now plainly seen. So it is with the Christian: the more the light of God enters his heart, the more he discovers the spiritual filth that dwells there. Beloved brother, or sister, it is not that you are becoming more sinful, but that God is now giving you a clearer and fuller sight of your sinfulness. Praise Him for it, for the eyes of the vast majority of your fellows (religionists included) are blind, and cannot see what so distresses you!

Second, side by side with sin in your heart is grace. There is a new and holy nature within the Christian as well as the old and unholy one. Grace is active within you, as well as sin. The new nature is influencing your conduct as well as the old. Why is it that you so desire to be conformed to the image of Christ, to trust Him fully, love Him fervently, and serve Him diligently? These longings do not proceed from the flesh. No, my distressed brother or sister, sin is not your complete master; if it were, all aspirations, prayers, and strivings after holiness would be banished from your heart. There are "as it were the company of two armies" (Song of Solomon 6:13) fighting to gain control of the Christian. As it was with our mother Rebekah—"the children struggled together within her" (Genesis 25:22)—so it is with us. But the very struggle shows that the issue is not yet decided. Had sin conquered, the soul would no longer be able to resist. The conqueror disarms his enemy so that he can no longer fight back. The very fact that you are still fighting proves that sin has not vanquished you! It may seem to you that it soon will; but the issue is not in doubt. Christ will yet save you from the very presence of sin.

Having sought in the above paragraphs to heed the injunction found in Hebrews 12:12-13 to "lift up the hands which hang down, and the feeble knees," and to make "straight paths" for the feet of God's little ones, "lest that which is lame be turned out of the way," let me again direct our attention unto those who have no doubt of their acceptance in Christ, and perhaps feel no personal need for what has been said above. The Lord declared that a tree is known by its fruits, so there cannot be anything wrong in examining the tree of our heart to ascertain what kind of "fruit" it is now bringing forth, and discover whether it is such as may proceed from mere nature, or that which can only issue from indwelling grace. It may at once be objected, "But nothing spiritual can issue from ourselves." From our natural selves, no, but from a regenerate person, yes. But how can an evil tree ever be any different? Christ said, "Make the tree good, and his fruit good" (Matthew 12:33). This is typed out by engrafting a new slip on an old stock.

All pretensions unto the present enjoyment of the assurance of faith by those whose daily lives are unbecoming the gospel are groundless. They who are confident of entering that eternal happiness that consists very much in a perfect freedom from all sin, but who now allow themselves in the practice of sin (persuading themselves that Christ has fully atoned for the same), are deceived. None truly desire to be free from sin in the future who do not sincerely long to forsake it in the present. He who does not pant after holiness here is dreadfully mistaken if he imagines that he desires holiness hereafter. Glory is but grace consummated; the heavenly life is but the full development of the regenerated life on earth. Neither death nor the second coming of Christ will effect any radical change in the Christian;

it will only perfect what he already has and is. Any, then, who pretend unto the assurance of salvation, boast of their pardon and present possession of eternal life, but who have no experience of deep sorrow for sin, real indignation against it, and hatred of themselves because of transgressions, know nothing at all of what holy assurance is.

In considering the basis of the Christian's assurance we must distinguish sharply between the ground of his acceptance before God and his own knowledge that he is accepted by Him. Nothing but the righteousness of Christ, wrought out by Him in His virtuous life and vicarious death, can give any sinner a perfect legal standing before the thrice holy God. And nothing but the communication of a new nature, a supernatural work of grace within, can furnish proof that the righteousness of Christ has been placed to my account. Whom God legally saves, He experimentally saves; whom He justifies, them He also sanctifies. Where the righteousness of Christ is imputed to an individual, a principle of holiness is imparted to him; the former can only be ascertained by the latter. It is impossible to obtain a scriptural knowledge that the merits of Christ's finished work are reckoned to my account except by proving that the efficacy of the Holy Spirit's work is evident in my soul.

"Wherefore the rather, brethren, give diligence to make your calling and election sure" (2 Peter 1:10). Why does he place "calling" before "election"? Here it is the converse of what we find in Romans 8:29-30: "Whom he did (1) predestinate, them he also (2) called"; but here in Peter the Christian is bidden to make sure (1) his "calling" and (2) his "election." Why this variation of order? The answer is simple. In Romans 8:29-30, it is the execution of God's eternal counsels; but in 2 Peter 1 it is the Christian's obtaining an experimental knowledge of the same. I have to work back from effect to cause, to examine the fruit so as to discover the nature of the tree. I have no immediate access to the Lamb's book of life; but if I obtain clear proof that I have been effectually called by God out of the darkness of sin's enmity into the light of reconciliation, then I know that my name is written there.

And how am I to make my calling and election sure? The context of this passage tells me very plainly. In verses 5-7 we read, "And beside this, giving all diligence, add to your faith virtue; and to virtue, knowledge; and to knowledge temperance; and to temperance, patience; and to patience, godliness; and to godliness, brotherly kindness; and to brotherly kindness, charity." There we have a summary of those graces that make up the Christian character. The word "add" signifies "supply in connection with," just as in a choir a number of parts and voices unite together in making harmony; or, as in a rainbow the various colors, side by side, blend into one beautiful whole. In the previous verses the apostle had spoken of the grace of God manifested toward His elect. By regeneration they had "escaped the corruption that is in the world through lust." Now he adds, Do not not rest satisfied with a negative salvation, but press forward unto perfection; be in thorough earnest to "add to your faith" these virtues. Faith is not to be alone, but the other spiritual graces must supplement and adorn it.

In verses 8-9 the Spirit moved the apostle to set before us the consequences of a compliance or a non-compliance with the duties specified in verses 5-7. The "these things" in verse 8 are the seven graces of the previous verses. If "all diligence" is devoted to the acquiring and cultivating of those lovely virtues, then a certain consequence is sure to follow; as cause stands to effect, so is fruitfulness dependent on Christian diligence. Just as the neglect of our daily food will lead to leanness and feebleness, just as lack of exercise means flabby muscles, so a disregard of the divine injunction of verse 5 issues in soul-barrenness, lack of vision, and loss of holy assurance. This brings us now to verse 10.

The "Wherefore the rather, brethren" of verse 10 points to a contrast from the sad tragedy presented in verse 9. There we see the pitiful results of being in a backslidden state of soul. There is no remaining stationary in the Christian life. He who does not progress retrogrades. He who does not diligently heed the divine precepts soon loses the good of the divine promises. He who does not add or conjoin with his faith the graces mentioned in verses 5-7 will soon fall under the power of unbelief. He who does not cultivate the garden of his soul will quickly find it grown over with weeds. He who neglects God's exhortations will lose the joy of his salvation, and will lapse into such a state of doubting that he will seriously question his divine sonship. To prevent this the apostle says, "Wherefore the rather, brethren, give diligence to make your calling and election sure."

The obvious meaning, then, of this exhortation in 2 Peter 1:10 is, stir yourselves, take pains to secure satisfactory evidence that you are among the effectually called and elect of God. Let there be no doubt or uncertainty about it; you profess to be a child of God, then justify your profession by cultivating the character and displaying the conduct of one. Sure proof is this that something more than a mere resting upon John 5:24 or Acts 16:31 is demanded of us! It is only in proportion as the Christian manifests the fruit of a genuine conversion that he is entitled to regard himself, and be regarded by others, as one of the called and elect of God. It is just in proportion as we add to our faith the other Christian graces that we have solid ground on which to rest the assurance we belong to the family of Christ. It is not those who are governed by self-will, but "as many as are led by the Spirit of God, they are the sons of God" (Romans 8:14).

Robert Hawker wrote in 1803: "In times so critical to the interests of vital religion, and amidst such awful departures from the faith as we are daily called upon to behold, it becomes a very anxious inquiry in the breasts of the humble: Is there no method under divine grace by which the believer may arrive to a well-grounded assurance, concerning the great truths of the gospel? Is it not possible for him to be so firmly settled in those great truths as that he shall not only be ready 'to give an answer to every one that asketh him a reason of the hope that is in him,' but to find the comfort of it in his own mind, that his faith 'doth not stand in the wisdom of men, but in the power of God'? To this inquiry I answer, Yes, blessed be God, there is. An infallible method is discovered, at once to secure from the possibility of apostasy, and to afford comfort and satisfaction to the believer's own mind, concerning the great truths of God; namely from the Spirit's work in the heart; by the sweet influences of which he may find 'joy and peace in believing, and abound in hope through the power of the Holy Spirit.'"

Christian assurance, then, is a scripturally-grounded knowledge that I am in the narrow way that leads unto life. Thus, it is based upon the Word of God, yet consists of the Holy Spirit's enabling me to discern in myself a character to which the divine promises are addressed. We have the same Word to measure ourselves by now as God will judge us by in the day to come. Therefore it behooves every serious soul to prayerfully and carefully set down the scriptural marks of God's children on the one side, and the characteristics of his own soul and life on the other, and determine if there is any real resemblance between them.

I will close this section by quoting from the saintly Samuel
Rutherford (1637):

> You may put a difference between you and reprobates if
> you have these marks: If you prize Christ and His truth so
> as you will sell all and buy Him, and suffer for it. If the
> love of Christ keeps you back from sinning more than the
> law or fear of hell does. If you are humble, and deny your
> own will, wit, credit, case, honor, the world, and the vanity
> and glory of it. Your profession must not be barren and
> void of good works. You must in all things aim at God's
> honor; you must eat, sleep, buy, sell, sit, stand, speak, pray,
> read, and hear the Word with a heart purpose that God
> may be honored. Acquaint yourself with daily praying;
> commit all your ways and actions to God by prayer, suppli-
> cation, and thanksgiving; and do not count it much if you
> are mocked, for Christ Jesus was mocked before you.

17

The Attainment of Assurance

In writing to a company of the saints, an apostle was inspired to declare, "Being confident of this very thing, that He which hath begun a good work in you will perform (or "finish") it until the day of Jesus Christ" (Philippians 1:6). That is what distinguishes the regenerate children of God from empty professors, from those who, while having a "name to live," are really spiritually dead (Revelation 3:1). This is what differentiates true Christians from deluded ones. And in what does this "good work" that is "begun" within the saved consist? It is variously described in different Scriptures. It is the heart being purified by faith (Acts 15:9). It is the love of God being shed abroad in the heart by the Holy Spirit (Romans 5:5). It is the laws of God being written on their hearts (Hebrews 8:10). Thus, the nature of Christian assurance is a well-founded knowledge that I am a child of God. The basis of this assurance is that there is an unmistakable agreement between my character, experience, and life, and the description that Holy Writ furnishes of the characters, experiences, and lives of God's children. Therefore, the attainment of assurance is by an impartial scrutiny of myself and an honest comparing of myself with the scriptural marks of God's children.

A reliable and satisfactory assurance cart only be attained or reached by means of a thorough self-examination. As Richard Baxter wrote in *The Saint's Everlasting Rest* in 1680:

"Oh, therefore, Christians, rest not till you can call this rest your own. Sit not down without assurance. Get alone, and bring thy heart to the bar of trial; force it to answer the interrogatories put to it; set the qualifications of the saints on one side and the qualifications of thy soul on the other side, and then judge what resemblance there is between them. Thou hast the same Word before thee by which to judge thyself now as thou shalt be judged by at the great day. Thou mayest there read the very articles upon which thou shalt be tried; try thyself by these articles now. Thou mayest there know beforehand on what terms men shall then be acquitted or condemned. Try now whether thou art possessed of that which will acquit thee, or whether thou be in the condition of those that will be condemned; and accordingly acquit or condemn thyself. Yet be sure thou judge by a true touchstone, and mistake not the scripture description of a saint, that thou neither acquit nor condemn thyself by mistake."

The need for such self-examination is indeed great, for multitudes are deceived; they are quite sure that they are Christians, yet they are without the marks of one. In a sermon on 1 Chronicles 4:10, Spurgeon said:

"They say they are saved, and they stick to it they are, and think it wicked to doubt it; but yet they have no reason to warrant their confidence. There is a great difference between presumption and full assurance. Full assurance is reasonable; it is based on solid ground. Presumption takes for granted, and with brazen face pronounces that to be its own to which it has no right whatever. Beware, I pray thee, of presuming that thou art saved. If thy heart be renewed, if thou shalt hate the things that thou didst once love, and love the things that thou didst once hate; if thou hast really repented; if there be a thorough change of mind in thee; if thou be born again—then thou hast reason to rejoice. But if

there be no vital change, no inward godliness; if there be
no love for God, no prayer, no work of the Holy Spirit,
then thy saying, 'I am saved,' is but thine own assertion,
and it may delude, but it will not deliver thee."

Oh, what efforts Satan puts forth to keep people from this
vitally important and all-necessary work of self-examination. He
knows full well that if many of his deceived victims set about the
task in earnest, they would soon discover that no miracle of divine grace has been wrought in them, and that this would cause
them to seek the Lord with all their hearts. He knows too that
real Christians would gain much advantage against the power of
indwelling sin would they but thoroughly search their own
hearts. Many are diverted from this wholesome work by the evil
example set by so many who now bear the name of Christ. Not
a few argue that if he or she (who claims to have been a Christian so much longer, and appears to know the Bible so much
better) who is so worldly, so governed by the "lust of the flesh,
and the lust of the eyes, and the pride of life," is sure he is
bound for heaven, why should I be concerned?

But the state of men's hearts is what holds so many back
from the discharge of this duty. Some are so ignorant that they
do not know what self-examination is, nor what a servant of
God means when he seeks to persuade them to "prove your own
selves" (2 Corinthians 13:5). Others are so much in love with
sin, and have such a dislike for the holy ways of God, they dare
not venture on the trial of their state lest they should be forced
from the course they so much relish to one that they hate. Others are so taken up with their worldly affairs, and are so busy
providing for themselves and their families, they say, "I pray
thee, have me excused" (Luke 14:18). Others are so slothful that
they cannot be induced on any consideration to be at those
pains that are necessary in order to know their own hearts.

Pride holds many back. They think highly of themselves. They are so sure of their salvation, so thoroughly convinced that all is right between their souls and God, they deem any search after proof and testing of themselves by Scripture to see if they have the marks of those who are "new creatures in Christ Jesus" as quite unnecessary and superfluous. They have been brought up in a religious atmosphere where none of those professing the name of Christ expressed any doubts about their state. They have been taught that such doubts are of the devil, a calling into question the veracity of God's Word. They have heard so many affirm, "I know that my Redeemer liveth," they felt it their duty to echo the same, forgetting that he who first uttered these words (Job 19:25) was one of whom God said, "There is none like him in the earth, a perfect and an upright man, one that feareth God, and escheweth evil" (Job 1:8).

Tens of thousands have been taught that it is wrong for the Christian to look within himself, and they have blindly followed the advice of such physicians "of no value." How can it be wrong for me to examine my heart to see whether or not God has written His laws upon it (Hebrews 8:10)? How can it be wrong for me to look and see whether or not God has begun a "good work" in me (Philippians 1:6)? How can it be wrong for me to test myself by the Parable of the Sower to see which of its four soils represents my heart? How can it be wrong to measure myself by the Parable of the Virgins, and ascertain whether or not the "oil" of regenerating and sanctifying grace is within the "vessel" of my soul (Matthew 25:4)? Since God Himself declares, "If any man have not the Spirit of Christ, he is none of His" (Romans 8:9), how can it be wrong for me to make sure that I am indwelt by Him?

Rightly did an eminent Puritan say, "The Scripture abounds in commands and cautions for our utmost diligence in our search and inquiry, whether we are made partakers of Christ or not, or whether His Spirit dwells in us or not; which argue both the difficulty of attaining an assured confidence herein, as also the danger of our being mistaken, and yet the certainty of a good issue upon the diligent and regular use of means to that purpose" (John Owen on Hebrews 3:14, 1670). Alas, this is what has been so strenuously opposed by many during the last two or three generations. An easy-going religion, well calculated to be acceptable unto the slothful, has been zealously propagated, representing the salvation of the soul and assurance of the same as a very simple matter.

It is very evident to one who has been taught of God that the vast majority of present-day evangelists, tract-writers, and "personal workers" do not believe one-half of what Holy Writ declares concerning the spiritual impotence of the natural man, or the absolute necessity of a miracle of grace being wrought within him before he can savingly turn to Christ. Instead, they erroneously imagine that fallen man is a "free moral agent," possessing equal power to accept Christ as to reject Him. They suppose all that is needed is information and coercion, to preach the gospel and persuade men to believe it. But have they never heard of the Holy Spirit? Oh, yes, and they say that they believe that only He can effectually convict of sin and regenerate. But do their actions agree with this? They certainly do not, for not only is there practically no definite waiting upon God and an earnest seeking from Him the power of His Spirit, but they sally forth and speak and write to the unsaved as if the Holy Spirit had no existence.

Now just as it is plainly implied by such "novices" that lost sinners can receive Christ any time they make up their minds to do so, just as they are constantly told that nothing more is needed than to believe that Christ died for them and rest on

John 3:16 and salvation is theirs, so the idea has been inculcated that the professing Christian may enjoy the full assurance of faith any time he wishes, and that nothing more is required for this than to "rest on John 5:24," and the like. One verse of Holy Scripture is sufficient to give the lie to this popular delusion: "The Spirit itself beareth witness with our spirit that we are the children of God" (Romans 8:16). If the written promises of God were sufficient of themselves to produce assurance, then what is there need for the third person of the Godhead to "bear witness" with the spirit of the Christian that he is a child of God?

As this verse is virtually given no place at all in modern ministry, let us ponder its terms. "The Spirit itself beareth witness with our spirit that we are the children of God." The clear implication of these words is that the actual existence of the saint's sonship is, at times at least, a matter of painful uncertainty, and that the supernatural agency of the Spirit is required to authenticate the fact, and thus allay all fear. To be fully assured of the amazing fact that God is my spiritual Father demands something more than the testimony of my own feelings or the opinions of men, and, let me reverently add, something more than resting upon a divine promise. Millions have rested on the words "this is My body," and no argument could persuade them that the bread upon the Lord's table was not actually changed into Christ's literal flesh.

Who is so competent to authenticate the work of the Spirit in the heart as the Spirit Himself? What, then, is the mode of His testimony? Not by visions and voices, nor by any direct inspiration or new revelation of truth. Not by bringing some verse of Scripture (of which I was not thinking) vividly before the mind, so that the heart is made to leap for joy. If the Christian had no surer ground than that to stand upon, he might well despair. Satan can bring a verse of Scripture before the mind (Matthew 4:6), and produce in his victims strong emotions of joy, and impart a false peace to the soul. Therefore the witness of the Spirit, to be decisive and conclusive, must be something that the Devil cannot duplicate. And what is that? It is this: Satan cannot beget divine grace and impart real holiness to the heart.

"The Spirit itself beareth witness with our spirit." To "bear witness with" is a legal term, and signifies to produce valid and convincing evidence. "Our spirit" here has reference to the renewed conscience. Concerning natural men it is said, "which show the work of the law written in their hearts, their conscience also bearing witness" (Romans 2:15). But the conscience of the natural man is partial, dim-sighted, and stupid. Grace makes it tender, pliant, and more able to do its office. The desire of the regenerate man, and unto which he exercises himself, is "to have always a conscience void of offense toward God, and toward men" (Acts 24:16). Where such a conscience is (by grace) maintained, we can say with the apostle, "Our rejoicing is this (what? resting on John 3:16? No, but) the testimony of our conscience, that in simplicity and godly sincerity. . .we have had our conversation in the world" (2 Corinthians 1:12).

Was the beloved Paul off the right track when he found something in himself that afforded ground for "rejoicing"? According to many present-day teachers, he was. It is a great pity that these men do not give less attention to human writings, and more to the Holy Scriptures, for then they would read, "The backslider in heart shall be filled with his own ways; and a good man shall be satisfied from himself" (Proverbs 14:14). If that text is despised because it is in the Old Testament, then we also read in the New Testament: "But let every man prove his own work, and then shall he have rejoicing in himself alone, and not in another" (Galatians 6:4). Once more, "Let us not love in word, neither in tongue; but in deed and in truth. And hereby we know that we are of the truth, and shall assure our hearts before Him" (1 John 3:18-19). What is the method that God here sets before His children for assuring their hearts before Him? Not in telling them to appropriate one of His promises, but to walk in the truth, and then their own spirit will bear witness to their divine sonship.

"The Spirit itself beareth witness with our spirit that we are the children of God." In addition to the testimony of a renewed conscience that is enjoyed by the Christian when he (by grace) is walking in the truth, the Spirit adds His confirmation. How? First, He has laid down clear marks in the Scriptures by which we may settle the question. "For as many as are led by the Spirit of God, they are the sons of God" (Romans 8:14). Why tell us this, if "resting on John 5:24" is all that is necessary? Second, by working such graces in the saints as are peculiar to God's children. In Galatians 5:22 these graces are expressly designated "the fruit of the Spirit." Third, by His spiritual consolation: "walking in the fear of the Lord, and in the comfort of the Holy Ghost" (Acts 9:31, cf. Romans 15:13). Fourth, by producing in the Christian the affections that dutiful children bear to a wise and loving parent (Romans 8:15).

To sum up, the blessed Spirit witnesses along with our spirit that we are the children of God by enabling us to discern (in the light of Scripture) the effects and fruits of His supernatural operation within us. The breathings of the renewed heart after holiness, the pantings after a fuller conformity to the image of Christ, and the strivings against sin, are all inspired by Him. Thus, by begetting in us the divine nature, by teaching us to deny "ungodliness and worldly lusts," and to "live soberly, righteously, and godly, in this present world" (Titus 2:12), the Spirit conducts us to the sure conclusion that we are the children of God. Thereby He shows us there is a real correlation between our experience and revealed truth. "Hereby know we that we dwell in Him, and He in us, because He hath given us of His Spirit" (1 John 4:13).

18

The Subjects of Assurance

Under this heading I propose briefly to consider the character of those persons to whom the privilege of Christian assurance rightfully belongs. Here again there are two extremes to be guarded against. On the one hand is that class of people who have been deceived by the slogan, "Believe you are saved, and you are saved," which is best met by pointing out that genuine assurance is never any greater than is our evidence of the same. On the other hand are those people who are fearful that such evidence is unattainable while the body of sin indwells them. To such I would ask, is it impossible to ascertain whether or not the health of your body is sound? Are there not certain symptoms and signs that are a clear index? If I were doubtful, and feared that some fatal disease was beginning to grip me, I would seek a physician. Were he merely to look at me and then lightly say, "Your health is good," I would leave him and seek another physician who was more competent. I would request a thorough overhauling—taking my blood pressure, the sounding of my heart, the testing of my other vital organs. So it should be with the soul.

In seeking to determine from God's Word who are entitled to Christian assurance, let us ask and answer a number of questions. Who are they with whom the great God dwells? "With him also that is of (not a haughty and boastful, but) a contrite and humble spirit" (Isaiah 57:15). "To this man will I look, even to him that is poor and of a contrite spirit, and trembleth at My Word" (Isaiah 66:2). Do you? Or do you joke over or argue about its sacred contents? Whom does God really forgive? They who "repent" and are "converted" (Acts 3:19), that is, they who turn their backs upon the world and sinful practices, and yield to Him; those in whose hearts God puts His "laws" and writes them in their minds, in consequence of which they love, meditate upon, and keep His commandments. Note how Hebrews 10:16 precedes 10:17!

Who is the man whom Christ likened unto one who built his house upon the rock? Not merely him who "believes," but "whosoever heareth these sayings of mine, and doeth them" (Matthew 7:24). Who are truly born again? "Every one that doeth righteousness" (1 John 2:29), they who love the brethren with such a love as is described in 1 John 3:17-18. To whom does God experimentally reveal the eternal purpose of His grace? "The secret of the Lord is with them that fear Him; and He will show them His covenant" (Psalm 25:14). "To him that ordereth his conversation aright will I show the salvation of God (Psalm 50:23). What are the identifying marks of a saving faith? One that "purifies their hearts" (Acts 15:9), "worketh by love" (Galatians 5:6), "overcometh the world" (1 John 5:4). Only thus may I know that my faith is a living and spiritual one.

The birth of the Spirit can only be known from its effects (John 3:8). Thus, it is by comparing what God, in His Word, has promised to do in His elect with what His Spirit has or has not wrought in my heart that I can ascertain whether assurance of salvation is my legitimate portion. This is "comparing spiritual things with spiritual" (1 Corinthians 2:13). Wondrous things has God prepared "for them that love Him" (1 Corinthians 2:9). How important it is, then, for me to make sure that I love Him. Many suppose that because they have (or had) a dread of eternal punishment that therefore they love God. Not so. True love for God is neither begotten by fears of hell nor hopes of heaven. If I do not love God for what He is in Himself, then I do not love Him at all! And if I love Him, my desire, my purpose, my aim will be to please Him in all things. Much might be added to this section of my subject, but I trust that sufficient has been said to enable exercised and honest souls to learn how to identify those whom Scripture teaches are entitled to the assurance of salvation.

19

Hindrances to Assurance

QUESTION 81: Are all true believers at all times assured of their present being in the estate of grace, and that they shall be saved?

ANSWER: Assurance of grace and salvation, not being of the essence of faith (2 Peter 1:10), true believers may wait long before they obtain it (1 John 5:13); and, after the enjoyment thereof, may have it weakened and intermitted, through manifold distempers, sins, temptations, and desertions (Psalm 77:7-9; 31:22); yet are they never left without such a presence and support of the Spirit of God as keeps them from sinking into utter despair (Psalm 73:13-15, 23; 1 John 3:9; Isaiah 54:7-11). *Westminster Confession of Faith, Larger Catechism.*

Just as the absence or loss of bodily health is not always attributable to the same cause or occasion, neither is the absence or diminution of assurance always to be accounted for in the same way; and just as any doctor who used only one medicine for the healing of all diseases would exhibit his crass incompetence, so any "Christian worker" who prescribes the same treatment to all soul-diseases at once declares himself a physician "of no value" (Job 13:4). There are degrees of health, both of body and soul; and this is to be ascribed, in the first place, to the high sovereignty of God, who distributes His gifts, both natural and spiritual, as He pleases. Yet, while we cannot impart health to ourselves, we should use legitimate means that, under God's

blessing, are conducive thereto. So too we may, through our sinful folly, undermine and destroy our health. The same holds
true in the spiritual realm.

In many cases, the lack of Christian assurance, or a very low
degree thereof, is due to a poor state of health. Bodily infirmi-
ties react on the mind. Low physical vitality is usually accompanied by lowness of spirits. A sluggish liver produces depression
and despondency. Many a person whose soul is now "cast
down" would be greatly benefited by more open-air exercise, a
change of diet, and a few doses of castor oil. Yet I am far from
saying that this course would result in the recovery or increase of
assurance, for spiritual effects cannot be produced by material
agents. Nevertheless, the removal of a physical hindrance is often an aid. Who can read the Word to profit while suffering
from a nerve-racking headache! What I wish to make clear is
that, in some instances at least, what is regarded as a lack of assurance is nothing more than physical inability to enjoy the
things of God. Nor do I mean by this that none are blessed with
the joy of the Lord while their bodily health is at a low ebb. Not
so. There are striking cases that show the contrary. But it still
remains that many are missing much spiritual good through
their disregard for the elementary laws of physical well-being.

The assurance of some of God's dear children has been hindered by a defective ministry. They have sat under teaching that
was too one-sided, failing to preserve a due balance between the
objective and the subjective aspects of the truth. They have been
encouraged to be far more occupied with self than with Christ.
Knowing that many are deceived, fearful lest they also should
be, their main efforts are directed to self-examination. Disgusted
too by the loud boastings of empty professors, perceiving the
worthlessness of the carnal confidence voiced by the frothy religionists all around them, they hesitate to avow the assurance of

salvation lest they be guilty of presumption or be puffed up by the devil. Yea, they have come to regard doubts, fears, and uncertainty as the best evidence of spiritual humility.

Now while I am by no means prepared to sanction the idea last named, yet I have no hesitation whatever in saying that I much prefer it to the presumptuous claims now being made by so many. Far rather would I cast my lot with a company of lowly, pensive, self-distrustful people who exclaim, "'Tis a point I long to know. Often it causes anxious thoughts such as, Do I love the Lord or not? Am I His, or am I not?," than fraternize with those who never have a doubt of their acceptance with Christ, but who are self-complacent and haughty, and whose daily walk compares most unfavorably with the former. It is far better to be weighed down by a sense of my vileness and go mourning all my days over lack of conformity to Christ, than to remain ignorant of my real state and go about light-hearted and light-headed, wearing a smile all the time.

But surely there is a happy medium between spending most of my days in Doubting Castle and the Slough of Despond, so that I am virtually a stranger to "the joy of the Lord," and experiencing a false peace from Satan that is never disturbed by the voice of conscience. Holy assurance and lowly heartedness are not incompatible. The same apostle who cried, "O wretched man that I am! Who shall deliver me from the body of this death?" (Romans 7:24), also declared, "I know whom I have believed, and am persuaded that He is able to keep that which I have committed unto Him" (2 Timothy 1:12). "As sorrowful, yet always rejoicing" (2 Corinthians 6:10) summed up his dual experience. We too are "sorrowful" daily if God has opened our eyes to see something of the mass of corruption that still indwells us; "sorrowful" too when we perceive how far, far short we come of the example that Christ has left us. Yet we also rejoice because God has not left us in ignorance of our dreadful state, that He has planted within us deep yearnings after holiness, and because we know these yearnings will be fully realized when we are freed from this body of death.

The assurance of other saints is greatly dampened by the assaults of Satan. There are three principal things that our great enemy seeks to accomplish. He seeks to incite us to sin, to hinder the exercise of our graces, and to destroy our peace and joy. If he fails largely in the first two, he is often very successful in the third. Posing as an angel of light, he comes to the soul preaching the holiness of God and the exceeding sinfulness of sin, his object being to overwhelm the conscience and drive to despair. He presses upon the Christian the awfulness and prevalence of his unbelief, the coldness of his heart toward God, and the many respects in which his deportment and actions are un-Christ-like. He reminds him of numerous sins, both of omission and commission, and the more tender is his conscience, the more poignant are Satan's thrusts. He challenges him to compare his character with that given of the saints in Scripture, and then tells him his profession is worthless, that he is a hypocrite, and that it is mockery to take the holy name of Christ upon his polluted lips.

So many succumb to Satan's efforts to disturb their peace and destroy their assurance through not knowing how to meet his attacks, and through forgetting that Scripture is very far from representing the earthly lives of God's children as flawless and perfect. As a general rule it is the best thing to acknowledge the truth of Satan's charges when he declares that I am still a great sinner in myself. When he asks me if such and such a lusting of the flesh is consistent with a heart in which a miracle of divine grace has been wrought, I should answer, "Yes, for the 'flesh' in me has neither been eradicated nor refined."

When Satan asks, "How can such doubts consist with a heart to which God has communicated saving faith?" you can remind him how Scripture tells us of one who came to Christ saying, "Lord, I believe; help Thou mine unbelief" (Mark 9:24).

But the most common hindrance to assurance is the indulgence of some known sin. When a Christian deliberately follows some course that God's Word forbids, when he lives in some unwarranted practice and God has often touched him for it, and his conscience has been sorely pricked and yet he perseveres in the same—then no wonder if he is destitute of assurance and the comfort of the Spirit. The cherishing of sin necessarily obscures the evidences of divine sonship, for it so abates the degree of our graces as to make them undiscernible. Allowed sin dims the eye of the soul so that it cannot see its own state, and stupefies the heart so that it cannot feel its own condition. But more, it provokes God, so that He withdraws from us the benevolent light of His countenance. "But your iniquities have separated between you and your God, and your sins have hid His face from you, that He will not hear" (Isaiah 59:2).

The sad history of David presents a solemn case in point. His fearful fall brought with it painful consequences. "When I kept silence, my bones waxed old through my roaring all the day long; for day and night Thy hand was heavy upon me. My moisture is turned into the drought of summer" (Psalm 32:3-4). But, blessed be God, his earthly life did not end while he was in this lamentable state. "I acknowledged my sin unto Thee, and mine iniquity have I not hid. I said, I will confess my transgressions unto the Lord; and Thou forgavest the iniquity of my sin" (Psalm 32:5).

Further light on the deep exercises of soul through which David passed is given us in Psalm 51. There we hear him crying, "Hide Thy face from my sins, and blot out all mine iniquities.

Create in me a clean heart, O God; and renew a right spirit within me. Cast me not away from Thy presence; and take not Thy Holy Spirit from me. Restore unto me the joy of Thy salvation" (vv. 9–12). This leads us to consider the maintenance of assurance.

20

Maintaining Assurance

Here again there are two extremes to be guarded against: the fatalistic lethargy of "I cannot help myself," and the humanistic effrontery which affirms that the remedy lies in my own hands. Spiritual assurance is a divine gift, nevertheless the Christian has a responsibility for preserving the same. It is true that I cannot speak peace to my own conscience, or apply the balm of Gilead to my wounded heart; yet I can do many things to grieve and repel the great Physician. We cannot bring ourselves near to God, but we can and do wander from Him. Of ourselves we cannot live for God's glory, but we can live for our own. Of ourselves we cannot walk after the Spirit, but we can walk after the flesh. We cannot make ourselves fruitful unto every good word and work, but we may by disobedience and self-indulgence bring leanness into our souls and coldness into our affections. We cannot impart health to our bodies, but we can use means that, by God's blessing, further the same.

1. Holy assurance cannot be maintained unless the Christian keeps his heart with "all diligence" (Proverbs 4:23). "Watch ye and pray lest ye enter into temptation" (Mark 14:38). "Take heed, brethren, lest there be in any of you an evil heart of unbelief, in departing from the living God" (Hebrews 3:12). As John Owen said, there must be "a watchful fighting, and contending against the whole work of sin, in its deceits and power, with all the contribution of advantage and efficacy that it hath from Sa-

tan and the world. This the apostle peculiarly applies it unto, in the cautions and exhortations given us, to take heed of it, that we be not hardened by it; seeing its whole design is to impair or destroy our interest and persistency in Christ, and so to draw us off from the living God."

More especially does the Christian need to pray and strive against presumptuous sins. Right hands must be cut off and right eyes plucked out (Matthew 5:29); a gangrened member must be amputated or death will soon ensue. Cry mightily unto God for enabling grace to mortify besetting sins. Remember that a deliberate running into the place of danger, a willful exposing of myself to sin's attacks, is a tempting of the Lord. "Enter not into the path of the wicked, and go not in the way of evil men. Avoid it, pass not by it, turn from it, and pass away" (Proverbs 4:14-15). Oh, what circumspect walking is called for in a world that abounds with pitfalls on every side!

2. Holy assurance cannot be maintained unless the Christian is diligent in cherishing his graces. A Christian is one who had been made a partaker of those spiritual graces that accompany salvation (Hebrews 6:9); and for the establishing of his comfort and joy it is necessary that he know himself to be in possession of them. The best evidence that we are in a state of grace is to grow in grace. As John Owen wrote, for this there needs to be a "daily constant cherishing, and laboring to improve and strengthen every grace by which we abide in Christ. Neglected grace will wither, and be ready to die (Revelation 3:2); yea, as to some degrees of it, and as to its work in evidencing the love of God unto us, or our union with Christ, it will utterly decay. Some of the churches in the Revelation had lost their first love as well as left their first works. Hence is that command that we should grow in grace, and we do so when grace grows and thrives in us. And this is done two ways:

"First, when any individual grace is improved. When that faith which was weak becomes strong, and that love which was faint and cold, becomes fervent and is inflamed; which is not to be done but in and by the sedulous exercise of these graces themselves, and a constant application of our souls by them to the Lord Christ. Second, by adding one grace unto another: 'and besides this, giving all diligence, add to your faith, virtue; to virtue, knowledge'; etc. (2 Peter 1:5); this is the proper work of spiritual diligence. This is the nature of gospel-graces, because of their linking together in Christ, and as they are wrought in us by one and the self-same Spirit, the exercise of one leads us to the stirring up and bringing in the exercise of another into the soul."

3. Assurance is maintained by keeping short accounts with God. "Let us draw near with a true heart in full assurance of faith, having our hearts sprinkled from an evil conscience, and our bodies washed with pure water" (Hebrews 10:22). Note the intimate connection there is between these things. There cannot be a sincere and hearty approach unto God as worshippers while the guilt of sin is resting upon our consciences. Nothing more effectually curtails our freedom in drawing nigh to the thrice Holy One than the painful realization that my conduct has been displeasing to Him. "Beloved, if our heart condemn us not, then we have confidence toward God" (1 John 3:21).

But strive as he may, walk as cautiously and carefully as he will, in many things the Christian offends (James 3:2) daily, both by sins of omission and commission. Yet, blessed be God, provision has been made by our loving Father even for this sad failure of ours. "If we confess our sins, He is faithful and just to forgive us our sins, and to cleanse us from all unrighteousness" (1 John 1:9). As soon as we are conscious of having done wrong, we should take ourselves to God, holding nothing back, but freely acknowledging each offence. Nor should we fear to do this frequently, daily, yea, constantly. If the Lord bids us to forgive our sinning brethren "until seventy times seven" (Matthew 18:22), is He less merciful? "He that covereth his sins shall not prosper; but whoso confesseth and forsaketh them (in heart and purpose) shall have mercy" (Proverbs 28:13).

4. Assurance is maintained by cultivating daily communion with God. "Our fellowship is with the Father, and with His Son Jesus Christ. And these things write we unto you, that your joy may be full" (1 John 1:3-4). Observe the connection between these two statements: fullness of joy (which, in this epistle, largely has reference to walking in the unclouded assurance of our divine sonship) is the fruit of fellowship with the Father and His Son. But what is signified by the term "fellowship"? Many seem to have but vague and visionary ideas of its meaning. Oneness of heart and mind, common interests and delights, unity of will and purpose, reciprocal love, is what is denoted. It is a fellowship "in the light" (1 John 1:5-7). This was perfectly realized and exemplified by the Lord Jesus. He walked in uninterrupted communion with the Father, delighting in His will (Psalm 40:8), keeping His commandments (John 14:31), always doing those things that were pleasing in His sight (John 8:29). And this very epistle declares: "He that saith he abideth in Him ought himself also so to walk, even as He walked" (2:6). What a standard is here set before us! Yet after it we should prayerfully and constantly strive.

Fellowship is participation in the light and love of God. It is refusing the things He hates and choosing the things in which He delights. It is losing my will in His. It is going out of self and embracing God in Christ. It is the acceptance of His estimate of things, thinking His thoughts after Him, viewing the world and all in it, life both present and future, from His viewpoint. It is therefore a being molded into conformity with His holy nature. It is living for His glory. And thus it is a fellowship of joy, and "the joy of the Lord is your strength" (Nehemiah 8:10)—strength to overcome temptations, to perform the duties of life, to endure its sorrows and disappointments. The closer we walk with the Lord, the brighter will be the evidences of our divine sonship.

Part 5

Dialogues

21

Dialogue With
Mr. Carnal Confidence

MR. CARNAL CONFIDENCE: Good morning, Mr. Editor, I wish to have a talk with you about those articles on '"Assurance" that you wrote.

THE EDITOR: Be seated, please. First of all, may I courteously but frankly inform you that my time is already fully occupied in seeking to minister unto God's dear children, yet I am never too busy to do all in my power to help a needy soul.

MR. CARNAL CONFIDENCE: Oh, I am not seeking help; my purpose in calling is to point out some things in your articles where I am quite sure you erred.

THE WRITER: It is written, dear friend, "If any man think that he knoweth any thing, he knoweth nothing yet as he ought to know" (1 Corinthians 8:2). Therefore I trust that God will ever give me grace to willingly consider and weigh the views of others, and receive through them anything He may have for me. Yet, on the other hand, I am not prepared to debate with any man upon divine things.

MR. CARNAL CONFIDENCE: Well, I am quite sure that I am right, and you are wrong, and I feel it my duty to tell you so.

THE WRITER: Very good, I am ready to listen to what you have to say, only reminding you again that I cannot enter into a debate with you, for the things of God are too holy to argue about; though a friendly discussion, in the right spirit, may prove mutually helpful. Before beginning, let us seek the help of the Holy Spirit, that He may graciously subdue the flesh in each of us, guide our conversation so that the words of our mouths and the meditations of our hearts may be acceptable in God's sight (Psalm 19:14), remembering that for every idle word each of us will yet have to give an account.

MR. CARNAL CONFIDENCE: I consider that in your articles you have made a very difficult and complicated matter out of what is really very simple. According to your ideas, a person has to go to a lot of trouble in order to discover whether or not he is saved, whereas if a man believes God's Word he may be sure in a moment.

THE WRITER: But are all those who believe God's Word really saved? Did not the Jews of Christ's day believe implicitly in the divine authorship of the Old Testament? Do not Russelites (Jehovah's Witnesses) and others today insist loudly upon their faith in the divine inspiration of the Bible? Does not the devil himself believe the same?

MR. CARNAL CONFIDENCE: That is not what I meant; my meaning is that if I rest upon some verse of Holy writ as God's promise to me, then I know He cannot disappoint me.

THE WRITER: That is just the same in principle. Does not the Romanist rest with full confidence upon that declaration of Christ's "this is My body"? Saving faith is not faith in the authenticity of any verse of Scripture, but rather faith in the Person of Him who gave us the Scriptures, faith in the Christ who is made known in the Scriptures.

MR. CARNAL CONFIDENCE: Yes, I know that, and I do believe in God and in His Son, and I know that I am saved because He says so.

THE WRITER: Where in Scripture does God say that you are saved?

Mr. CARNAL CONFIDENCE: In John 5:24, in Acts 16:31, and many other places.

THE WRITER: Let us turn to these passages, please. In John 5:24 the Lord Jesus describes one who has passed from death unto life. He tells us two things about that individual, that serve to identify him. First, "he that heareth My word." That is definite enough. But of course it means far more than simply listening to His Word with the outward ear.

MR. CARNAL CONFIDENCE: Ah, right there you want to mystify what is simple, and perplex souls with what is quite clear.

THE WRITER: Pardon me, you are mistaken. I only wish to rightly understand the words God has used, and to do this it is necessary to carefully compare Scripture with Scripture and discover how each word is used by the Spirit.

MR. CARNAL CONFIDENCE: I object; that may be all right for you, but common people do not have the leisure for deep study. God knew this, and has written His word in plain language that ordinary folk can understand. "Hear" means "hear," and that is all there is to it.

THE WRITER: I believe you are quite sincere in what you have said, and you have expressed the view that a great many hold today. But, if you will allow me to say so, it is a very defective one. God places no premium upon laziness. God has so ordered things that nothing is obtained without diligence and industry. Much work and care has to be devoted to a garden if anything is obtained from it. The same holds good everywhere else: what time and trouble is required to keep our bodies in working order! Can, then, the eternal concerns of our souls be more lightly dismissed or more easily secured? Has not God

bidden us "Buy the truth" (Proverbs 23:23)? Has He not plainly
told us "If thou criest after knowledge, and liftest up thy voice
for understanding; if thou seekest her as silver, and searchest for
her as for hid treasures; then thou shalt understand the fear of
the Lord, and find the knowledge of God" (Proverbs 2:3-5)?

Mark how the Israelites were fed of old in the wilderness
(Exodus 16). God did not provide them with baked loaves of
bread ready to eat. No, instead, He gave the manna from
heaven, which was a small round thing (v. 14). Work and patience were called for in order to gather (v. 17) it. Note too
when the sun waxed hot, it melted (v. 21), so that they had to
get up early to secure it! Moreover, the manna would not keep:
"let no man leave of it till the morning." It bred worms and
stank (vv. 19-20) if they tried to preserve it for another day.
Then, after it had been gathered, the manna had to be ground
in mills or beaten in a mortar, and baked in pans and made into
cakes (Numbers 11:8). All of this typified the fact that if a soul is
to eat the Bread of life, he must devote himself in earnest, and,
as Christ says, 'Labor . . . for that meat which endureth unto
everlasting life'" (John 6:27).

Thus it is in connection with the obtaining of a right understanding of any verse of Scripture: pains have to be taken with
it, patience has to be exercised, and prayerful study engaged in.
Returning to John 5:24: the one who has passed from death
unto life, says Christ, is "he that heareth My word." Let us turn
then to other passages where this term is found. "They are
turned back to the iniquities of their forefathers, which refused
to hear My words" (Jerermiah 11:10). "Because ye have not
heard My words, behold, I will send and take all the families of
the north" (Jeremiah 25:8-9). See also Jeremiah 35:17; Zechariah 1:4; Matthew 7:24; John 10:27. In all of these verses, and in
many others that might be given, to "hear" means to heed what

God says, to act upon it, to obey Him. So he who hears the voice of Christ heeds His command to turn away from all that is opposed to God and become in subjection to Him.

MR. CARNAL CONFIDENCE: Well, let us turn to Acts 16:31; that is simple enough. There is no room allowed there for any quibbling. God says, "Believe on the Lord Jesus Christ and thou shalt be saved." God says that to me. I have believed on Christ, and so I must be saved.

THE WRITER: Not so fast, dear friend. How can you prove God says that to you? Those words were spoken under unusual circumstances, and to a particular individual. That individual had been brought to the end of himself; he was deeply convicted of his sins; he was in terrible anguish of soul; he had taken his place in the dust, for we are told that he came trembling, and fell down before Paul and Silas (Acts 16:29). Now is it fair to take the words of the apostles to such a man and apply them indiscriminately to anybody? Are we justified in ignoring the whole setting of that verse, wrenching it from its context, and giving it to those who have not any of the characteristics which marked the Philippian jailor?

MR. CARNAL CONFIDENCE: I refuse to allow you to browbeat me, and move me from the simplicity of the gospel. John 3:16 says, "For God so loved the world, that He gave His only begotten Son, that whosoever believeth in Him should not perish, but have everlasting life." Now I have believed on the Son, and therefore am fully assured that I possess eternal life.

THE WRITER: Are you aware of the fact that in this same Gospel of John we are told "Many believed in His name, when they saw the miracles which He did. But Jesus did not commit Himself unto them" (John 2:23-24)? There were many who believed in Christ who were not saved by Him (see John 8:30, and note verse 59! John 12:42-43! There is a believing in Christ that

saves, and there is a believing in Him that does not save; and
therefore it behooves every sincere and earnest soul to diligently
examine his "faith" by Scripture and ascertain which kind it is.
There is too much at stake to take anything for granted. Where
eternal destiny is involved, surely no trouble can be too great for
us to make sure.

MR. CARNAL CONFIDENCE: I am sure, and no man can
make me doubt.

THE WRITER: Is your faith purifying your heart (Acts
15:9)? Is it evidenced by those works that God requires (James
2:17)? Is it causing you to overcome the world (1 John 5:4)?

MR. CARNAL CONFIDENCE: Oh, I don't claim to be
perfect, but I know whom I have believed, and am persuaded
that He is able to keep that which I have committed unto Him
against that day.

THE WRITER: I did not ask if you were perfect; but have
you been made a new creature in Christ? Have old things passed
away, and all things become new (2 Corinthians 5:17)? Are you
treading the path of obedience? For God's Word says, "He that
saith, 'I know Him,' and keepeth not His commandments, is a
liar, and the truth is not in him" (1 John 2:4).

MR. CARNAL CONFIDENCE: I am not occupied with
myself, but with Christ. I am not concerned about my walk, but
with what He did for poor sinners.

THE WRITER: To be "occupied with Christ" is rather a
vague expression. Are you occupied with His authority? Have
you surrendered to His Lordship? Have you taken His yoke
upon you? Are you following the example that He has left His
people? Christ cannot be divided. He is not only Priest to be
trusted, but is also Prophet to be heeded, and King to be subject
unto. Before He can be truly "received," the heart must be emptied of all those idols that stand in competition with Him. It is

not the adulation of our lips, but the affection of our souls that He requires; it is not an intellectual assent, but the heart's surrender to Him that saves.

MR. CARNAL CONFIDENCE: You are departing from the simplicity of the gospel; you are making additions unto its one and only stipulation. There is nothing that God requires from the sinner except that he believe on the Lord Jesus Christ.

THE WRITER: You are mistaken. The Lord Jesus said, "Repent ye, and believe the gospel" (Mark 1:15).

MR. CARNAL CONFIDENCE: That was before the Cross, but in this dispensation repentance is not demanded.

THE WRITER: Then, according to your ideas, God has changed the plan of salvation. But you err. After the Cross, Christ charged His disciples, "That repentance and remission of sins should be preached in His name among all nations" (Luke 24:47). If we turn to the book of Acts we find that the apostles preached repentance in this dispensation. On the day of Pentecost, Peter bade the convicted Jews to repent (2:38). Reviewing his ministry at Ephesus, Paul declared that he had testified both to the Jews and also to the Greeks "repentance toward God, and faith toward our Lord Jesus Christ" (Acts 20:21); while in 17:30 we are told that God "now commandeth all men every where to repent."

MR. CARNAL CONFIDENCE: Then do you insist that if a person has not repented, he is still unsaved?

THE WRITER: Christ Himself says so. "Except ye repent, ye shall all likewise perish" (Luke 13:5). So, too, if a man has not been converted, he is yet unsaved. "Repent ye therefore and be converted, that your sins may be blotted out" (Acts 3:19). There must be an about-face; there must be a turning from Satan unto God, from the world unto Christ, from sin unto holiness. Where that has not taken place, all the believing in the world will not save one. Christ saves none who is still in love with sin; but He is ready to save those who are sick of sin, who long to be cleansed from its loathsome foulness, who yearn to be delivered from its tyrannizing power. Christ came here to save His people from their sins.

MR. CARNAL CONFIDENCE: You talk to me as though I were the helpless slave of strong drink or some other appetite; but I want you to know I was never the victim of any such thing.

THE WRITER: There are other lusts in fallen man besides those that break forth in gross outward sins—such as pride, covetousness, selfishness, self-righteousness—and unless they are mortified, they will take a man to hell as surely as will profanity, immorality, or murder. Nor is it enough to mortify these inordinate affections. The fruit of the Spirit, the graces of godliness, must also be brought forth in the heart and life; for it is written, "follow peace with all men, and holiness, without which no man shall see the Lord" (Hebrews 12:14). And therefore it is a pressing duty for each of us to heed the divine exhortation, "Examine yourselves, whether ye be in the faith; prove your own selves. Know ye not your own selves, how that Jesus Christ is in you, except ye be reprobates?" (2 Corinthians 13:5).

Notice very carefully, dear friend, that the one point pressed upon the Corinthians was "that Jesus Christ is in you," and not their trusting that He died for them. Just as the Christian can only discover that his name was written in the Book of Life before the foundation of the world by discerning that God has written His laws on his heart (Hebrews 10:16), so I can ascertain that Christ died for me only by making sure that He now lives in me. And it is obvious that if the Holy One indwells me then His presence must have wrought a radical change both in character and in conduct. This, above everything else, is what I sought to make clear, and emphasized in my articles on "Assur-

ance," namely the imperative necessity of our making sure that
the Lord Jesus occupies the throne of our hearts, has the supreme place in our affections, and regulates the details of our
lives. Unless this is the case with us, then our profession is vain,
and all our talk of trusting in Christ's finished work is but idle
words.

MR. CARNAL CONFIDENCE: I consider all you have said
to be but the language of a Pharisee. You are occupied with your
own fancied goodness and are delighting in your own worthless
righteousness.

THE WRITER: Pardon me, but I rather rejoice in what
Christ's Spirit has wrought in me, and pray that He will carry
forward that work of grace to the glory of His name. But we
must bring our discussion to a close. I would respectfully urge
you to attend unto that exhortation addressed to all professing
Christians, "Give diligence to make your calling and election
sure" (2 Peter 1:10).

MR. CARNAL CONFIDENCE: I shall do nothing of the
sort. I hate the very word "election." I know that I am saved,
though I do not measure up to the impossible standard you
want to erect.

THE WRITER: Fare thee well; may it please the Lord to
open your blind eyes, reveal to you His holiness, and bring you
to His feet in godly fear and trembling.

22

Dialogue With
Mr. Humble Heart

MR. HUMBLE HEART: Good morning, sir. May I beg the favor of an hour of your valuable time?

EDITOR: Come in, and welcome. What can I do for you?

MR. HUMBLE HEART: I am sorely troubled in spirit. I long so much to be able to call God my Father, but I fear I might be guilty of lying were I to do so. There are many times when I have a little hope that He has begun a good work within me, but, alas, for the most part, I find such a mass of corruption working within that I feel sure I have never been made a new creature in Christ. My heart is so cold and hard toward God that it seems impossible the Holy Spirit could have shed abroad God's love in me; unbelief and doubts so often master me that it would be presumptuous to think I possess the faith of God's elect. Yet I want to love Him, trust Him, and serve Him; but it seems I cannot.

EDITOR: I am very glad you called. It is rare indeed to meet with an honest soul these days.

MR. HUMBLE HEART: Excuse me, sir, but I do not want you to form a wrong impression of me. An honest heart is the very blessing I crave, but I am painfully conscious, from much clear evidence, that I do not possess it. My heart is deceitful above all things, and I am full of hypocrisy. I have often begged

God to make me holy, and right after my actions proved that I did not mean what I said. I have often thanked God for His mercies, and then have soon fretted and murmured when His providence crossed my will. I had quite a battle before I came here to see you tonight as to whether I was really seeking help, or as to whether my secret desire was to win your esteem—and I am not sure now which was my real motive.

To come to the point, sir, if I am not intruding, I have read and re-read your articles on "Assurance" that appeared earlier in this book. Some things in those articles seemed to give me a little comfort, but other things almost drove me to despair. Sometimes your description of a born-again soul agreed with my own experience, but at other times I seemed as far from measuring up to it as the north and south poles are asunder. So I do not know where I am. I have sought to heed 2 Corinthians 13:5 and examine myself, and, when I did so, I could see nothing but a mass of contradictions; or, it would be more accurate to say, for each one thing I found that seemed to show that I was regenerate, I found ten things to prove that I could not be so. And now, sir, I'm mourning night and day, for I feel of all men the most miserable.

EDITOR: Hypocrites are not exercised about their motives, nor troubled over the deceitfulness of their hearts! At any rate, I am thankful to see you so deeply concerned about your soul's eternal interests.

MR. HUMBLE HEART: Alas, sir, I am not half as much concerned about them as I ought to be. That is another thing that occasions me much anguish. When the Lord Jesus tells us that the human soul is worth more than the whole world put together (Mark 8:36), I feel that I must be thoroughly blinded by Satan and completely under the dominion of sin, seeing that I am so careless. It is true that at times I am alarmed about my state and fearful that I shall soon be in hell; at times, too, I seem to seek God more earnestly and read His Word more diligently. But, alas, my goodness is "as a morning cloud, and as the early dew it goeth away" (Hosea 6:4). The cares of this life soon crowd out thoughts of the life to come. O sir, I want reality, not pretense; I want to make sure, yet I cannot.

EDITOR: That is not so simple a task as many would have us believe.

MR. HUMBLE HEART: It certainly is not. I have consulted several Bible-teachers, only to find them "physicians of no value" (Job 13:4). I have also conferred with some who boasted that they never have a doubt, and they quoted to me Acts 16:31, and on telling them I believed they cried, "Peace, peace," but there was no peace in my heart.

EDITOR: Ah, dear friend, it is not without reason that God has bidden us "give diligence to make your calling and election sure" (2 Peter 1:10). And even after we have given diligence, we still need the Holy Spirit to bear witness with our spirit that we are the children of God (Romans 8:16). Moreover, spiritual assurance may easily be lost, or at least be clouded, as is evident from the case of him who wrote the 23rd Psalm; for at a later date he had to cry unto God, "Restore unto me the joy of Thy salvation."

EDITOR: Before proceeding further, had we not better seek the help of the Lord? His holy Word says, "In all thy ways acknowledge Him, and He shall direct thy paths" (Proverbs 3:6). And now, dear brother, for such I am assured you really are, what is it that most causes you to doubt that you have passed from death unto life?

MR. HUMBLE HEART: My inward experiences, the wickedness of my heart, the many defeats I encounter daily.

EDITOR: Perhaps you are looking for perfection in the flesh.

MR. HUMBLE HEART: No, hardly that, for I know the "flesh," or old nature, is still left in the Christian. But I have met with some who claim to be living "the victorious life," who say they never have a doubt, never a rising of anger, discontent, or any wicked feelings or desires; that Christ so controls them that unclouded peace and joy is theirs all the time.

EDITOR: Bear with me if I speak plainly, but such people are either hypnotized by the devil or they are fearful liars. God's Word says, "If we say that we have no sin, we deceive ourselves, and the truth is not in us" (1 John 1:8). And again, "There is not a just man upon earth that doeth good, and sinneth not" (Ecclesiastes 7:20). And again, "In many things we offend all" (James 3:2). The beloved Apostle Paul, when well advanced in the Christian life, declared, "I find then a law that, when I would do good, evil is present with me. For I delight in the law of God after the inward man, but I see another law in my members, warring against the law of my mind, and bringing me into captivity to the law of sin which is in my members" (Romans 7:21-23).

MR. HUMBLE HEART: That relieves my mind somewhat, yet it scarcely reaches the root of my difficulty. What troubles me so much is this: when God regenerates a man, he becomes a new creature in Christ Jesus. The change wrought in him is so great that it is termed a "passing from death unto life." It is obvious that if God the Holy Spirit dwells in a person, there must be a radical difference produced, both inwardly and outwardly, from what he was before. Now it is this that I fail to find in myself. Instead of being any better than I was a year ago, I feel I am worse. Instead of humility filling my heart, so often pride rules it; instead of lying passive like clay in the Potter's hand to be molded by Him, I am like a wild ass's colt; instead of rejoicing in the Lord always, I am frequently filled with bitterness and repinings.

EDITOR: Such experiences as you describe are very sad and humbling, and need to be mourned over and confessed to God. They must never be excused or glossed over. Nevertheless, they are not incompatible with the Christian state. Rather are they so many proofs that he who is experimentally acquainted with the "plague of his own heart" (1 Kings 8:38) is one in experience with the most eminent of God's saints. Abraham acknowledged that he was "dust and ashes" (Genesis 18:27). Job said, "I abhor myself" (42:6). David prayed, "Have mercy upon me, O Lord; for I am weak. O Lord, heal me; for my bones are vexed" (Psalm 6:2). Isaiah exclaimed, "Woe is me, for I am undone; because I am a man of unclean lips" (6:5). In the anguish of his heart Jeremiah asked, "Wherefore came I forth out of the womb to see labor and sorrow, that my days should be consumed with shame?" (20:18). Daniel once owned, "There remained no strength in me, for my comeliness was turned in me into corruption" (Daniel 10:8). Paul cried, "O wretched man that I am! Who shall deliver me from the body of this death?" (Romans 7:24).

One of the principal things that distinguishes a regenerate person from an unregenerate one may be likened unto two rooms that have been swept, but not dusted. In one, the blinds are raised and the sunlight streams in, exposing the dust still lying on the furniture. In the other, the blinds are lowered, and one walking through the room would be unable to discern its real condition. Thus it is in the case of one who has been renewed by the Spirit: his eyes have been opened to see the awful filth that lurks in every corner of his heart. But in the case of the unregenerate, though they have occasional twinges of conscience when they act wrongly, they are very largely ignorant of the awful fact that they are a complete mass of corruption unto the pure eyes of the thrice holy God. It is true that an unregenerate person may be instructed in the truth of the total depravity of fallen man, and he may "believe" the same, yet his belief does not humble his heart, fill him with anguish, make him loathe himself, and feel that hell is the only place that is fit for him to dwell in. But it is far otherwise with one who sees light in God's light (Psalm 36:9); he will not so much as lift up his eyes to heaven, but smites upon his leprous breast, crying, "God be merciful to me, the sinner."

MR. HUMBLE HEART: Would you kindly turn to the positive side, and give me a brief description of what characterizes a genuine Christian?

EDITOR: Among other gifts, every real Christian has such a knowledge of God in Christ, as works by love, that he is stirred up to earnestly inquire after the will of God, and studies His Word to learn that will, having a sincere desire and making an honest endeavor to live in the faith and practice of it.

MR. HUMBLE HEART: I cannot boast of my knowledge of God in Christ, yet by divine grace this I may say, that I desire no other heaven on earth than to know and to do God's will, and be assured that I have His approval.

EDITOR: That is indeed a good sign that your soul has been actually renewed, and doubtless He who has begun a work of grace in your heart will make the great change manifest in your life and actions. No matter what he thinks or says, no unregenerate man really desires to live a life that is pleasing to God.

MR. HUMBLE HEART: God forbid that I should flatter myself, yet I hope I have often found delight when reading God's Word or hearing it preached, and I do sincerely meditate upon it, and long that I may grow in grace. Yet at times, I am tempted with vain and vile thoughts, and I strive to banish them, my heart rising up against them; yet sometimes I yield to them. I loathe lying and cursing, and cannot endure the company of those who hate practical godliness; yet my withdrawal from them seems nothing but pharisaical hypocrisy, for I am such a miserable failure myself. I pray to God for deliverance from temptation, and for grace to resist the devil, but I fear that I do not have His ear, for more often than not I am defeated by sin and Satan.

EDITOR: When you thus fail in your duty, or fall into sin, what do you think of yourself and your ways? How are you affected therewith?

MR. HUMBLE HEART: When I am in this deplorable condition, my soul is grieved; my joy of heart and peace of conscience gone. But when I am a little recovered out of this sinful lethargy, my heart is melted with sorrow over my folly; and I address myself to God with great fear and shame, begging Him to forgive me, pleading 1 John 1:9, and humbly imploring Him to "renew a right spirit within me."

EDITOR: And why is it that you are so troubled when sin conquers you?

MR. HUMBLE HEART: Because I truly wish to please the Lord, and it is my greatest grief when I realize that I have dishonored and displeased Him. His mercy has kept me, thus far, from breaking out into open and public sins, yet there is very much within which I know He hates.

EDITOR: Well, my dear brother and companion in the path of tribulation, God has ordained that the Lamb shall be eaten with "bitter herbs" (Exodus 12:8). So it was with the apostle: "As sorrowful, yet always rejoicing" (2 Corinthians 6:10) summed up his dual experience—sorrowful over his sinful failures, both of omission and commission, yet rejoicing over the provisions that divine grace has made for us while we are in this dreary desert. The Mercy-seat is ever open to us, where we may draw near, unburden our heavy hearts, and pour out our tale of woe; the Fountain that has been opened for sin and for uncleanness (Zechariah 13:1), where we may repair for cleansing. I am indeed thankful to learn that your conscience confirms what your tongue has uttered. You have expressed enough to clearly evidence that the Holy Spirit has begun a good work in your soul. But I trust you also have faith in the Lord Jesus, the Mediator, by whom alone any sinner can draw near unto God.

MR. HUMBLE HEART: By divine grace I do desire to acknowledge and embrace the Lord Jesus upon the terms on which He is proclaimed in the gospel, to believe all His doctrine as my Teacher, to trust in and depend upon the atoning sacrifice that He offered as the great High Priest, and to submit to His rule and government as King. But, alas, in connection with the last, "to will is present with me, but how to perform that which is good I find not" (Romans 7:18).

EDITOR: No real Christian ever attains his ideal in this life; he never reaches that perfect standard that God has set before us in His Word, and that was so blessedly exemplified in the life of Christ. Even the Apostle Paul, near the close of his life, had to say, "Not as though I had already attained, either were already perfect, but I follow after, if that I may apprehend that for which also I am apprehended of Christ Jesus" (Philippians 3:12). But may I ask if you are sensible of how you arrived at the good desires you mentioned? Do you suppose that such a disposition is natural to you, or that it has resulted from your own improvement of your faculties?

MR. HUMBLE HEART: No, sir, I dare not ascribe to nature that which is the effect and fruit of divine grace. If I have any measure of sanctification (which is what I long to be assured of), then it can only be by the gift and operation of God. I am too well acquainted with my wretched self. I know too well that by nature I am alive to vanity and sin, but dead to God and all real goodness; that folly possesses my soul, darkness shrouds my understanding; that I am utterly unable to will or to do what is pleasing in God's sight, and that my natural heart is set contrary to the way of salvation proposed in the gospel, rising up against its flesh, condemning precepts and commandments. I see, I know, I feel that in me, that is in my flesh, there dwells no good thing.

EDITOR: Then do you realize what must be the outcome if God were to leave you unto yourself?

MR. HUMBLE HEART: Yes, indeed. Without the assistance of His Holy Spirit, I would certainly make shipwreck of the faith. My daily prayer is, "Hold Thou me up, and I shall be safe" (Psalm 119:117). My earnest desire is that I may watch and pray against every temptation. There is nothing I dread more than apostatizing, relaxing in my duty, returning to wallow in the mire.

EDITOR: These are all plain evidences of the saving grace of God at work within you, which I beseech Him to continue, so that you may be preserved with a tender conscience, work out your own salvation with fear and trembling, and obtain a full assurance of His love for you.

MR. HUMBLE HEART: I thank you kindly, sir, for your patience and help. What you have said makes me feel lighter in heart, but I wish to go home and prayerfully ponder the same, for I dare take no man's word for it. I want God Himself to say unto my soul, "I am thy salvation" (Psalm 35:3). Will you not pray that it may please Him to do so?

EDITOR: You shall certainly have a place in my feeble petitions. The Lord be very gracious unto you.

23

Dialogue 2 With Mr. Humble Heart

In communicating His Word, God was pleased to speak "at sundry times and in divers manners" (Hebrews 1:1). In the Scriptures of Truth we have clear doctrinal instruction and plain precepts for the regulation of conduct, but we also find dark parables and mysterious symbols. Side by side are history and allegory, hymns of praise and practical proverbs, precious promises and intricate prophecies. Variety stamps all the works and ways of God. This illustrates a principle that should guide those whom the Lord has called to teach His Word: there should be variety both in the matter of their messages and the methods employed in delivering them. Many are unable to apprehend abstract statements; comparatively few have minds trained to follow a course of logical reasoning. The teacher, then, ought to adapt himself to the capacity of his hearers. Blessedly do we find this exemplified in the ministry of the perfect Teacher. The teaching of the Lord Jesus was largely by question and answer. Having this in mind, I feel it may be wise to follow the last two articles on "Assurance" by another one in dialogue form.

EDITOR: Good evening, friend Humble Heart.

BROTHER HUMBLE HEART: Good evening, Mr. Editor. This is a pleasant surprise, for I was not expecting to be favored with a visit from one of God's servants. I do not feel worthy of their notice.

EDITOR: According to my promise, I have been seeking to remember you before the Throne of Grace; and while in prayer this morning there was impressed on my mind those words, "lift up the hands which hang down, and the feeble knees" (Hebrews 12:12). 1 have been impressed of late by that lovely prophetic picture of Christ found in Isaiah 40:11: "He shall feed His flock like a shepherd. He shall gather the lambs with His arm, and carry them in His bosom, and shall gently lead those that are with young." The Savior devotes special care and tenderness upon the weak of the flock, and in this He has left an example that the under-shepherds need to follow.

BROTHER HUMBLE HEART: It is indeed kind of you, sir, to bestow any trouble upon such a poor, worthless creature as I am. I would have thought your time had been more profitably employed in ministering to those who can take in the truth quickly, and who grow in it by leaps and bounds. As for me, I am so dull and stupid, so full of doubts and fears, that your labors on me are wasted.

EDITOR: Ah, my friend, all is not gold that glitters. The great majority of those who take the truth in quickly only do so intellectually; it has no power over the heart. And those who grow by leaps and bounds grow too swiftly for it to be real, or worth anything spiritually. Truth has to be bought (Proverbs 23:23): bought by frequent meditation thereon, by taking it home unto ourselves, by deep exercises of conscience, by wrestling with God in prayer, that He would apply it in power to the soul.

BROTHER HUMBLE HEART: Yes, I realize that, and it makes me feel so bad because God's Word has not been written on my heart. I have gone over in my mind, again and again, all that you said at our last meeting, and I am sure that I am unregenerate.

EDITOR: What leads you to such a conclusion?

BROTHER HUMBLE HEART: This, if I had been regenerated the Holy Spirit would be dwelling within me, and in that case He would be producing His blessed fruit in my heart and life. It is written, "The fruit of the Spirit is love, joy, peace, longsuffering, gentleness, goodness, faith, meekness, temperance, and self-control" (Galatians 5:22-23). And as I have endeavored to examine and search myself, I discover in me the very opposite of these heavenly graces.

EDITOR: God's workings in grace and His ways in the material creation have much in common, and if we observe closely the latter, we may learn much about the former. Now in the natural realm the production of fruit is often a slow process. Glance out now at the trees, and how do they look? They are lifeless and seem to be dead. Yet they are not; the vital sap is still in their roots, even though no signs of it are apparent to us. But in a little while, under the genial warmth of the sun, those trees will be covered with blossoms. Then, after a few days, those pretty blossoms will all have disappeared, blown off by the winds. Nevertheless, if those trees are examined closely it will be found that where those blossoms were are now little green buds. Many weeks have to pass before the owner of those trees is gladdened by seeing the buds develop into fruit.

A further lesson may be learned from our gardens. The orchard teaches us the need for patience; the garden instructs us to expect and overcome disappointments. Here is a bed, that has been carefully prepared and sown with seed. Later, the seed springs up and the plants appear from which the flowers are to grow. But side by side there spring up many weeds too. The uninstructed gardener was not expecting this, and is apt to be discouraged. Before he sowed the flower seed he thought he had carefully rooted up every nettle, thistle, and obnoxious plant; but now the bed has in it more weeds than flowers. So it is, my brother, with the heart of the Christian. Though the incorruptible seed of God's Word is planted there (1 Peter 1:23), yet the heart—neglected all through the years of unregeneracy—is overgrown with weeds (the lusts of the flesh), and to the anointed eye the heart looks more like the devil's weed plot than "the king's garden" (2 Kings 25:4).

BROTHER HUMBLE HEART: What you have just referred to in the natural realm is quite obvious, but I am not so clear about the spiritual application. Does not your last illustration belittle the work and power of the Holy Spirit? You have often quoted in your articles that Christ saves His people "from their sins" (Matthew 1:21). How, then, can any person rightfully regard himself as saved while he is conscious that many sins still have dominion over him?

EDITOR: I am glad you raised this point, for many dear souls are often troubled over it. Concerning the work and power of the Holy Spirit, light is thrown on this by various expressions that God has used in His Word. For example, in 2 Corinthians 1:22 (cf. Ephesians 1:13–14), we read that God has given the earnest of the Spirit in our hearts. Now an "earnest" means a part, and not the whole—an installment, as it were. The fullness of the Spirit's power and blessing is communicated to no Christian in this life. So again in Romans 8:23: "ourselves also, which have received the firstfruits of the Spirit"—a pledge, a sample only, of future greater abundance.

Let me call your attention to the words that immediately follow those just quoted from Romans 8:23, namely "even we ourselves groan within ourselves," which is the more striking because this same thing is seen again in 2 Corinthians 5:4–5. So those who are indwelt by the Spirit of God are a "groaning" people! It is true that the unregenerate groan at times, when suf-fering great bodily pain or over some heavy loss; but the groan-ing of the Christian is occasioned by something very different. He groans over the remains of depravity still left within him, over the flesh so often successfully resisting the Spirit, over see-ing around him so much that is dishonoring to Christ. This is clear from Romans 7:24 and Philippians 3:18.

BROTHER HUMBLE HEART: But only a few days ago I mentioned some of these very scriptures to one whom I regard as an eminent saint, and he told me that he had gotten out of Romans 7 and into Romans 8 long ago.

EDITOR: But as we have seen, the Christian in Romans 8 groans (v. 23)!

BROTHER HUMBLE HEART: The one I had reference to laughed at me for my doubts and fears, and told me I was dis-honoring God by listening to the devil.

EDITOR: It is much to be feared that he is a complete stranger to those exercises of heart that are experienced by every regenerate soul, and knows nothing of that heart-anguish and soul-travail that always precedes spiritual assurance. The Lord Jesus did not laugh at fearing souls, but said, "Blessed are they that mourn." It is clear that your acquaintance does not under-stand your case.

BROTHER HUMBLE HEART: But do you mean to say that all of God's children are as wretched in soul as I am?

EDITOR: No, I would not say that. The Holy Spirit does not give the same degree of light on the exceeding sinfulness of sin to all alike, nor does He reveal so fully unto all their own inward depravity. Moreover, just as God has appointed different seasons to the year, so no true Christian is always the same in his soul; there are cheerful days of spring and gloomy days of autumn, both in the natural and in the spiritual. "But the path of the just is as the shining light, that shineth more and more unto the perfect day" (Proverbs 4:18), nevertheless, "We must through much tribulation enter into the kingdom of God" (Acts 14:22). Both are true, though we are not always conscious of them both.

BROTHER HUMBLE HEART: I do not believe that any real Christian is ever plagued as I am, plagued so often with a spirit of rebellion, with unbelief, with pride, with such vile thoughts and desires that I would blush to mention them.

EDITOR: Ah, my brother, few unregenerate souls would be honest enough to acknowledge as much! The very fact that these inward workings of sin plague you is clear proof that you are regenerate, and there is within you a nature or principle of holiness which loathes all that is unholy. It is this that causes the Christian to groan, nevertheless this brings him into fellowship with the sufferings of Christ. While here the Lord Jesus was "the Man of sorrows," and that which occasioned all His grief was sin—not His own, for He had none, but the sins of others. This then is one reason why God leaves the sinful nature in His people even after regeneration, so that mourning over it they may be conformed to their suffering Head.

BROTHER HUMBLE HEART: But how does this tally with Christ's saving His people from their sins?

EDITOR: Matthew 1:21 in no way clashes with what I have been saying. Christ saves His people from the guilt and punishment of their sins, because that was transferred to and vicariously suffered by Him. He saves us too from the pollution of sin: His Spirit moves us to see, grieve over, confess our sins, and plead the precious blood; and as this is done in faith, the conscience is cleansed. He also saves us from the reigning power of sin, so that the Christian is no longer the absolute and abject slave of sin and Satan. Moreover, the ultimate fulfillment of this blessed promise (like that of many others) is yet future; the time is coming when the Lord Jesus shall rid His people of the very presence of sin, so that they shall be done with it forever.

BROTHER HUMBLE HEART: While on that point I wish you would explain to me those words "sin shall not have dominion over you" (Romans 6:14).

EDITOR: Observe first what that verse does not say. It is not, "sin shall not haunt and harass you," or, "sin shall not trip you and occasion many a fall." Had it said that, every Christian might well despair. To "have dominion over" signifies the legal right to command another, such as a parent over his child, or as one nation has over another that has been completely conquered in war. Such legal "dominion" sin does not have over any Christian. Christ alone is his rightful Lord. But sin oftentimes usurps authority over us, yet even experimentally it does not have complete dominion. It can lead no Christian to apostatize, that is, utterly and finally renounce Christ. It can never so dominate the believer that he is thoroughly in love with sin and does not repents when he offends.

BROTHER HUMBLE HEART: Thank you; but may I ask another question? Why is it that some of God's children are not plagued by sin as I am?

EDITOR: How can you be sure that they are not? "The heart knoweth his own bitterness" (Proverbs 14:10).

BROTHER HUMBLE HEART: But I can tell from their peaceful countenances, their conversation, their joy in the Lord, that it cannot so be the case with them.

EDITOR: Some are blessed with a more cheerful natural disposition than others. Some keep shorter accounts with God, making it a point of conscience to confess every known sin to Him. Some are more diligent in using the means of grace. They who neglect the reading of God's Word, meditation thereon, and approach the throne of grace only occasionally and formally, cannot expect to have healthy souls.

BROTHER HUMBLE HEART: I admit I cannot meet your arguments. What you say is doubtless true of God's people, but my case is far worse than you realize. I have such a sink of iniquity within, and so often find myself listless toward all that is spiritual, that I greatly fear there can be no assurance for me.

EDITOR: It is the devil who tells you that.

BROTHER HUMBLE HEART: How can one distinguish between the harassing doubts that the devil injects, and the convictions of sin and piercings of conscience that the Holy Spirit produces?

EDITOR: By the effects produced. Satan will tell you that it is no use to resist indwelling sin any longer, and that it is useless to pray any more. He seeks to produce despair, and tells many harassed souls they might as well commit suicide and put an end to their misery. But when the Holy Spirit convicts a Christian, He also works in his heart a godly sorrow, and moves him to acknowledge his transgressions to God. He leads to the throne of grace and gives again a sight of the cleansing blood of Christ; and this not once or twice, but to the end of our earthly lives. "For a just man falleth seven times, and riseth up again" (Proverbs 24:16). If then this agrees with your own experience, you must be a Christian.

BROTHER HUMBLE HEART: I cannot but be struck with the fact that your counsel and instruction is the very opposite of what was given to me by the last person I spoke to about my sorrows. He is a man very wise in the Scriptures, having scores of passages at his finger's end. He told me that the only way to get rid of my doubting was to believe the Word, and that every time I felt miserable to lay hold on one of the promises.

EDITOR: I think I know the company to which that man belongs. All they believe in is a natural faith, which lies in the power of the creature, a faith that is merely the product of our own will-power. But that is not the "faith of God's elect." Spiritual faith is the gift of God, and only the immediate operation of the Holy Spirit can call it forth into action in any of us. Shun such a people, my brother. Avoid all who give no real place to the Holy Spirit, but would make you believe that the remedy lies in your own "free-will." Seek more the company and communion of God Himself, and beg Him for Christ's sake to increase your faith and stay your mind upon Himself.

24

Brother Humble Heart's Spirits Lifted

BROTHER HUMBLE HEART: Good evening, Mr. Editor. I trust 1 am not intruding.

EDITOR: No, indeed, you are very welcome, Brother Humble Heart, and I am thankful to see from your countenance that your heart is lighter (Proverbs 15:13).

BROTHER HUMBLE HEART: I am glad to say it is so at present, for the Lord has been very gracious to me, and I cannot but think that it is in answer to your prayers, for the Scriptures declare, "The effectual fervent prayer of a righteous man availeth much" (James 5:16).

EDITOR: If the Lord has deigned to hear my feeble intercessions on your behalf, all the praise alone to Him. But tell me something of His goodness towards you.

BROTHER HUMBLE HEART: May it please the Lord to direct my thoughts, anoint my lips, and help me to do so. My story is rather a long one, but I will be as concise as the case allows.

A poor woman, known among the Lord's people as Sister Fearing, was left a widow some months ago, and having buried all her children, I knew she had no one to spade her garden. So this spring I called on her, and asked if she would allow me to do it.

EDITOR: I am glad to hear that; if godliness is not intensely practical, then it is only a name without the reality. It is written, "Pure religion and undefiled before God and the Father is this, to visit the fatherless and widows in their affliction, and to keep himself unspotted from the world" (James 1:27). And did this poor sister avail herself of your kind offer?

BROTHER HUMBLE HEART: Yes, with tears running down her face she told me she was quite unable to express her gratitude. After a while she said that it was not so much my offer to help that moved her so deeply, but that it gave her a little hope she was not completely abandoned by God.

I asked her why she ever entertained the thought that God had cast her off. She told me that most of the time she felt herself to be such a vile and polluted creature that a holy God could not look with any complacency upon her. She said she was so constantly tormented by doubts and fears that God must have given her over to an evil heart of unbelief. She added that, in spite of all her reading of the Word and crying unto the Lord for strength, her case seemed to grow worse and worse, so that it appeared heaven must be closed against her.

EDITOR: And what reply did you make to her sorrowful complaint?

BROTHER HUMBLE HEART: Why, there flowed into my mind a verse that I had not thought of for a long time. I felt it was from the Lord, and, looking to Him for wisdom and tenderness, I addressed the dear soul as follows:

Sister Fearing, I think you are too hasty in your conclusion. I have been just where you now are. I read in God's Word, "the kingdom of God is not in word, but in power" (1 Corinthians 4:20), and I reasoned that if God had set up His kingdom in my heart, then the power of sin would be broken. But, alas, I found sin in me stronger than ever. I read, "He that dwelleth in love dwelleth in God, and God in him" (1 John 4:16), but I could not believe He dwelt in me while I was in such bondage to slavish fear. I read, "Ye have received the Spirit of adoption, whereby we cry, 'Abba, Father' " (Romans 8:15), but I could not cry, "Abba, Father," so I was afraid God had nothing to do with me. I read, "Whosoever is born of God doth not commit sin" (1 John 3:9), and though I was preserved from bringing public reproach upon the name of Christ, yet I found myself continually overcome by sin within. My guilty conscience daily condemned me, and unto peace I was a stranger.

SISTER FEARING: You have accurately described my sad lot; but go on please.

BROTHER HUMBLE HEART: Suffer me, then, to ask you a few honest questions. Have you been chastised, rebuked, and made tender and sore for sin? And after feeling God's reproofs, was your spirit revived and refreshed under the Word, so that you hoped for better days?

SISTER FEARING: Yes, I have been conscious of God's rod upon me, and have owned with David, "Thou in faithfulness hast afflicted me" (Psalm 119:75). And there have been times, all too brief, when it seemed that I was softened and revived, and had a little hope; but the sun was soon again hidden behind dark clouds.

BROTHER HUMBLE HEART: Well, that proves that God does dwell within you, for He declares, "Thus saith the high and lofty One that inhabiteth eternity, whose name is Holy, I dwell in the high and holy place, and with him also that is of a contrite and humble spirit, to revive the spirit of the humble, and to revive the heart of the contrite ones" (Isaiah 57:15)!

SISTER FEARING: Yes, I am familiar with that verse, but it makes the case against me, for had God truly revived me, the effects of it would remain; instead, I am dry and parched, lifeless and barren.

BROTHER HUMBLE HEART: Again you are too hasty in writing bitter things against yourself (Job 13:26). Such revivings of faith, hope, and love in the soul are evidences of the Spirit's indwelling. But let me now give you the verse that flowed into my mind at the beginning of our conversation, for it exactly fits your case: "And now for a little space grace hath been showed from the Lord our God to leave us a remnant to escape, and to give us a nail in his holy place, that our God may lighten our eyes, and give us a little reviving in our bondage" (Ezra 9:8). Ah, dear sister, do you not see that this "little reviving," even though it is for "a little space," is a manifestation of God's dwelling in a broken and contrite heart?

EDITOR: That was indeed a word in season, and evidently given you by the Spirit. There are many hindered from enjoying assurance through unnecessary fears; because sin is in them as an active and restless principle, they imagine they have no contrary principle of holiness; and because in part they are carnal, judge that they are not spiritual. Because grace is but feebly active, they conclude they are void of it; and because for a long season they do not enjoy strong consolation, they suppose they have no title to it. They fail to distinguish between the motions of the flesh and the motions of the spirit. As surely as sin manifests the flesh to be in us, so does grieving over it, striving against it, repenting for it, and confessing it to God show the spirit or new nature indwells us. The Christian's sighs and groans are among his best evidences that he is regenerate.

BROTHER HUMBLE HEART: May I ask exactly what you meant when you said that many are hindered from enjoying assurance through unnecessary fears? My reason for asking is because in Philippians 2:12 God bids His people work out their salvation with fear and trembling.

EDITOR: Your question is well taken. We must distinguish sharply between the fears of godly jealousy and the fears of unbelief; the one is a distrusting of self, the other is a doubting of God; the former is opposed to pride and carnal confidence, the latter is the enemy of true peace. The eleven apostles manifested the fear of godly jealousy when the Savior announced that one would betray Him, and each of them inquired, "Lord, is it I?" David gave way to the fear of unbelief when he said, "I shall now perish one day by the hand of Saul" (1 Samuel 27:1). But I have interrupted your narrative; tell me how Sister Fearing responded to your giving her Ezra 9:8.

BROTHER HUMBLE HEART: Really, it seemed to make little impression. She sighed deeply, and for a while said nothing. Then she continued, "I fear it would be presumption for me to say that I have ever been revived, for a dead soul cannot be—he must first be quickened. Probably the raising of my spirits under the reading or hearing of the Word is nothing more than the joy of the stony-ground hearer" (Matthew 13:20-21).

I replied, "But one who has never been quickened has no pantings after God, never seeks Him at all, but seeks to banish Him entirely from his thoughts. True, he may go to church, and keep up a form of godliness before others, but there is no diligent seeking after Him in private, no yearnings for communion with Him.

"Perhaps, dear sister, it may be a day of 'small things' (Zechariah 4:10) with you. Often there is life where there is not strength. A child may breathe and cry, yet cannot talk or walk. If God is the object of your affection, if sin is the cause of your grief, if conformity to Christ is the longing of your heart, then a good work has begun in you (Philippians 1:6). If it is indwelling sin that makes you so wretched from day to day, if it is deliverance from its polluting effects you yearn and pray for, if it is the lustings of the flesh you are struggling against, then it must be because a principle of holiness has been implanted in your heart. Such godly exercises are not in us by nature; they are the products of indwelling grace. Despair not, for it is written of Christ, 'A bruised reed shall He not break, and the smoking flax shall He not quench' " (Matthew 12:20).

SISTER FEARING: Yes, it is one thing to understand these things intellectually, but it is quite another for God to apply them in power to the heart. That is what I long for, and that is what I lack. My wound is far too deadly for any man to heal. Oh, that I could be sure as to whether my disrelish of sin arises from mere natural convictions of conscience that every ungodly person feels more or less, whether they are suggestions from Satan for the purpose of deceiving me, or whether they actually are the strivings of the new nature against the old. Nothing short of the personal, mighty, and saving power of the Holy Spirit realized in my heart will or can give me genuine relief.

BROTHER HUMBLE HEART: I am thankful to hear you say this. Human comforts may satisfy an empty professor, but such a plaster will not heal one of the elect when stricken by God. It is His purpose to cut off every arm of flesh from them, to strip them and bring them, in their helplessness, as empty-handed beggars before the throne of His grace. As to whether or not the life of God is actually planted in the soul, therein lies the grand mystery; that is the pivot on which eternal destiny must turn. And no verdict from man can satisfy on that point. Only the Lord Himself can give such a testimony or witness as will satisfy one of His children. But when He does shine into the soul, when He applies His Word in power, when He says, "Thy sins are forgiven thee, go in peace," then no word from a preacher is needed. The Lord keep you at His feet till He grants this.

Until very recently I too was much exercised over the great danger of Satan instilling a false peace, and making me believe that all was well when it was not so; as I was also much perplexed to know how to distinguish between the convictions of natural conscience and the exercises of a renewed conscience. But the Lord has shown me that as a tree is known by its fruits, so the nature of a cause may be determined by the character of the effects it produces. They who are deluded by the false peace that Satan bestows are filled with conceit, presumption, and carnal confidence; they do not beg God to search them, being so sure of heaven they consider it quite unnecessary. The convictions of natural conscience harden, stop the mouth of prayer, and lead to despair. The convictions of a renewed conscience produce penitent confession, lead to Christ, and issue in honesty and uprightness before God.

In conclusion, let me earnestly counsel you, dear sister, to have nothing to do with those who profess their experience to be all peace and joy, and who, if you ask them whether they are tormented by the plague of their own heart, or whether they have felt the blood of Christ applied to their own conscience, laugh, and say they have nothing to do with feelings, but live above them. Such deluded creatures can be of no more help to a groaning saint than one suffering anguish from bodily ills would receive any relief from the so-called Christian Scientists, who tell him his pains are mental delusions, and tell him to think only of health and happiness. One and another are equally physicians of no value. Instead, pour out your woes into the ears of the great Physician, and in His own perfect time He will pour oil and wine into your wounds, and put a new song into your mouth.

Since then I have said nothing more to her on the subject, believing it best to leave her alone with God.

EDITOR: I am glad to hear that. None but blind zealots will attempt to do the Holy Spirit's work for Him. Much damage is often done to souls trying to force things. When God begins a work, we may safely leave it in His hands to continue and complete the same. And how happy am I, dear brother, to perceive the dew of the Spirit upon your own soul. It appears that "the winter is past, the rain is over and gone; the flowers appear." And "the time of the singing of birds is come" (Song of Solomon 2:11-12) with you.

BROTHER HUMBLE HEART: Thanks be unto God for taking pity upon such a wretch. It is much better with me now. The strange thing is, though, I had little or no real assurance myself when I commenced speaking to Sister Fearing, but as she mentioned the different things that so troubled her, God seemed to put into my mouth the very words most needed. And as I spoke them to her, He sealed them unto my own heart.

EDITOR: Yes, it is as we read in Proverbs 11:25: "The liberal soul shall be made fat: and he that watereth shall be watered also himself." In communicating the Word of God to His children, our own hearts are refreshed and our own faith is established. To him who uses what he has shall more be given.

I have long perceived the truth of what the apostle says in 2 Corinthians 1:4: "Who comforteth us in all our tribulation, that we may be able to comfort them which are in any trouble, by the comfort wherewith we ourselves are comforted of God." It is God's way to take His people, and especially His servants, through trying and painful experiences, in order that they may use to His glory the consolation wherewith He has comforted them. It is those who know most of the plague of their own heart who are best fitted to speak a word in season to weary souls. It is "out of the abundance of the heart the mouth speaketh," and it is he who has passed through the furnace who can best deal with those now in the fire. Let us pray that it may please God to be equally gracious unto Sister Fearing.

Other Titles Published by the Northampton Press

Sermons on the Lord's Supper, by Jonathan Edwards. 280 pp. Hardback

Heaven Taken by Storm, by Thomas Watson. 120 pp. Hardback

Sermons on Important Doctrines, by John Colquhoun. 240 pp. Hardback

Light and Heat: The Puritan View of the Pulpit, by Bruce Bickel 188 pp. Hardback

The Christian Father's Present to His Children, by John Angell James. 312 pp. Hardback

Saving Faith, by John Colquhoun. 296 pp. Hardback

The Christian on the Mount, by Thomas Watson. 128 pp. Hardback

Why Read the Puritans Today? by Don Kistler. 20 pp. Paperback

Distinguishing Traits of Christian Character, by Gardiner Spring. 144 pages. Hardback

For more information, or to order, go to
www.northamptonpress.org